DATE DUE	
DEC 2 6 2015	
FEB 0 6 2016	
JUL 2 0 2016	
	PRINTED IN U.S.A

CRIPPLED AMERICA

★ ★ ★

How to Make America Great Again

Donald J. Trump

THRESHOLD EDITIONS

New York   London   Toronto   Sydney   New Delhi

Threshold Editions
An Imprint of Simon & Schuster, Inc.
1230 Avenue of the Americas
New York, NY 10020

First Threshold Editions hardcover edition November 2015

THRESHOLD EDITIONS and colophon are trademarks of Simon & Schuster, Inc.

For information about special discounts for bulk purchases, please contact Simon & Schuster Special Sales at 1-866-506-1949 or business@simonandschuster.com.

The Simon & Schuster Speakers Bureau can bring authors to your live event. For more information or to book an event, contact the Simon & Schuster Speakers Bureau at 1-866-248-3049 or visit our website at www.simonspeakers.com.

Manufactured in the United States of America

10 9 8 7 6 5 4 3 2 1

Library of Congress Cataloging-in-Publication Data is available.

ISBN 978-1-5011-3796-9
ISBN 978-1-5011-3798-3 (ebook)

This book is dedicated to my parents, Mary and Fred C. Trump,
and my brothers and sisters—Maryanne, Robert, Elizabeth, and Fred.
Also, my wonderful wife, Melania, and my incredibly supportive children,
Don Jr., Ivanka, Eric, Tiffany, and Barron.

And importantly, to the people who are ready
to Make America Great Again!

CONTENTS

YOU GOTTA BELIEVE

SOME READERS MAY BE wondering why the picture we used on the cover of this book is so angry and so mean looking. I had some beautiful pictures taken in which I had a big smile on my face. I looked happy, I looked content, I looked like a very nice person. My family loved those pictures and wanted me to use one of them. The photographer did a great job.

But I decided it wasn't appropriate. In this book we're talking about Crippled America. Unfortunately, there's very little that's nice about it. So I wanted a picture where I wasn't happy, a picture that reflected the anger and unhappiness that I feel, rather than joy. Because we are not in a joyous situation right now. We're in a situation where we have to go back to work to make America great again. All of us. That's why I've written this book.

People say that I have self-confidence. Who knows?

When I began speaking out, I was a realist.

I knew the relentless and incompetent naysayers of the status quo would anxiously line up against me:

The politicians who talk a great game in campaigns—and play like total losers when they try to actually govern.

The lobbyists and special interests with their hands in our pockets on behalf of their clients.

The members of the media who are so far lost when it comes to being fair that they have no concept of the difference between "fact" and "opinion."

The illegal immigrants who have taken jobs that should go to people here legally, while over 20 percent of Americans are currently unemployed or underemployed.

Congress, which has been deadlocked for years and virtually unable to deal with any of our most pressing domestic problems, or even the most basic ones, such as passing a budget.

Meanwhile, the bedrock of this country—the middle class—and those 45 million Americans stuck in poverty have seen their incomes decline over the past 20 years. Understandably, their disenchantment and frustration at what's happening grows every day.

And even our lawyers and judges, the reflective "wise men," have been stepping all over the US Constitution, the bulwark of our democracy. They have recklessly appointed themselves to be policy makers, because our actual elected officials are paralyzed by partisanship.

As for the presidency and the executive branch, the incompetence is beyond belief.

As I write this, Russian president Vladimir Putin is totally outmaneuvering our president by putting together a coalition in Syria that will make Putin the only effective leader in the world. He and his allies—most notably Iran—have positioned themselves exactly where President Obama and our military have failed miserably for years.

We've wasted literally trillions of dollars in the Middle East, with virtually nothing to show for it except for alienating our best ally, Israel. To make matters worse, we've negotiated a worthless and costly nuclear treaty with Iran (now Russia's best friend) on the supposition that it will lead to greater harmony and world peace.

The idea of American Greatness, of our country as the leader of the free and unfree world, has vanished.

Despite all of these challenges—and actually because of the challenges—I decided to do something about it. I couldn't stand to see what was happening to our great country. This mess calls for leadership in the worst way. It needs someone with common sense and business acumen, someone who can truly lead America back to what has made us great in the past.

We need someone with a proven track record in business who understands greatness, someone who can rally us to the standard of excellence we once epitomized and explain what needs to be done.

When I started speaking out, I had no idea what the reaction would be. I know I'm a great builder, but I hadn't fully exposed my political thoughts and ideas to restore America's greatness.

I also knew that the Trump brand is one of the world's great icons of quality and excellence. Our buildings and resorts now stand very proudly (and beautifully) all over the United States and in many other countries.

I started with the issue of illegal immigration, and proposed building a major wall that would be very high and completely impervious to the flood of immigrants who we don't want or need here illegally.

Suddenly, Americans started to wake up to what was going on with regard to illegal immigration. Despite the large number of candidates who were running for the Republican nomination, what I was saying started to really hit home with people.

I started drawing crowds so large that we had to move our rallies into football stadiums. The first national debate drew 24 million viewers, which set a record for cable television. Despite some of the ridiculous, antagonistic questions—or maybe because of them—I fought back as I always do and began to explain my vision. As a result, most people thought I won the debate.

People were applauding. All of a sudden, people who had never cared about elections or never voted were rushing to our rallies.

The media, the politicians, and the so-called leaders of our country reacted in horror. But I persevered and went directly to the people, because I don't need anyone's financial support, nor do I need anyone's approval of what I say or do. I just had to do the right thing.

I have now begun to fill in some of the details of my vision. I've released a tax plan that gives the middle class and those with lower incomes a chance to keep more of what they earn, while restructuring how the richest Americans will be paying taxes.

I've committed to a truly more powerful military, one prepared and equipped to stand up to any and all of our foes. When we draw a line in the sand, it needs to mean something to all—especially our enemies.

I've introduced a whole new approach to job creation by encouraging companies to bring more of their jobs and manufacturing back to America, along with the trillions of dollars currently being held in foreign banks.

I've explained why Obamacare is a costly, ludicrous solution to our health care woes and one which must be repealed and replaced with a much better option. We need to fix the problem by creating competition in the private sector between insurance companies, and by allowing patients to choose the family doctors they want.

Competition is a magic word in education as well. Parents should have the right to choose the schools where their kids can get the best education. The weaker schools will be closed, and ineffective teachers will be fired. One-size-fits-all education—Common Core—is bad. Education should be locally based.

Domestically, we need to undertake a massive rebuilding of our infrastructure. Too many bridges have become dangerous, our roads are decaying and full of potholes, while traffic jams are costing millions in lost income for drivers who have jobs in congested cities. Public transit is overcrowded and unreliable and our airports must be rebuilt.

I could go on and on regarding many of the ideas I've written about in this book, and more that will be forthcoming. But let me add that while my critics are pushing their policy agendas, the last thing we need are more plans that evaporate after the elections.

What we need is leadership that can deal with our mess and begin to apply practical solutions to our problems. My goal is not to design hundreds of pages of government regulation and red tape like others propose. We need to outline commonsense policies and then knock some heads together if necessary to make them work.

I know how to deal with complex issues and how to bring together all the various elements necessary for success. I've done it for years and have built a great company and a massive net worth.

This book is designed to give the reader a better understanding of me and my ideas for our future. I'm a really nice guy, but I'm also passionate and determined to make our country great again.

It's time we turn America around from despair and anger to joy and accomplishment. It can happen, and it will happen.

Our best days still lie ahead. There is so much untapped greatness in our country. We're rich in natural resources, and we're rich in human talent.

Enjoy this book—and together, let's make America great again!

1

★　★　★

WINNING AGAIN

AMERICA NEEDS TO START winning again.

Nobody likes a loser and nobody likes to be bullied. Yet, here we stand today, the greatest superpower on Earth, and everyone is eating our lunch. That's not winning.

We have a president who tries to get tough and draw a line in the sand, but when that line gets crossed, there are no repercussions.

And when we try to negotiate with foreign countries? We don't stand up. We don't threaten to walk away. And, more important, we don't walk away. We make concession after concession. That's not winning.

If I ran my business that way, I'd fire myself.

Take one of the worst agreements in our history—the nuclear "treaty" with Iran—which John Kerry negotiated and

President Obama rammed through and around Congress. (Or, rather, he convinced his party to support it and filibuster any debate or vote on it.) This is probably the most important treaty of our time, and our very stupid leaders in Washington, DC, couldn't even bring themselves to hold a discussion and vote on it.

Ronald Reagan said, "Trust but verify"—but in this case we aren't following either piece of advice. How can we trust a man like the Ayatollah Khamenei? Just a month before we approved the treaty, he reiterated that his country was pledged to destroy and eliminate Israel, our most important ally and longtime partner in preserving some semblance of stability in the region. And as for verification, we don't even know what side-deals the International Atomic Energy Agency has struck with Iran. Or if we do know, they haven't been made public.

That's not winning—that's criminal negligence, in my view.

Then when every Senate Republican criticized this deal (and some of the Democrats did as well), the president compared his critics to our adversaries.

In other words, he sells out his friends and allies, and then defends his treaty by comparing his critics to our enemies.

That's what we call successful diplomacy?

Now we're going to open the gates to refugees from places like Syria, which is like extending a personal invitation to ISIS members to come live here and try to destroy our country from within.

This is America today, the shining city on a hill, which other countries used to admire and try to be like.

So what can be done about it? How do we start winning again?

To start with, we need a government that is committed to winning and has experience in winning. This book is about how we do that.

★

In early September 2015, I spoke at a major rally in Washington, DC. I told them that we need a military that will be so strong that we won't have to use it. And then I asked, "Are you listening, President Obama?" Almost everyone in the crowd cheered, but I understand why some of them were skeptical. Americans are used to hearing the same old promises from the same tired politicians who never produce any results, let alone any victories. I should know. For years I gave money—lots of money—to candidates from both parties who made personal pleas for my support for their campaigns. They promised to change things with new ideas and bring government back to its original, more limited purpose of protecting our country and putting our people first.

Candidate after candidate made all kinds of pledges like this, and very little, if anything, was done. How many of those problems have been solved? Nothing seemed to move forward in Washington.

Look at Congress, which has an understandably negative reputation among Americans.

And why not? They do nothing.

They can't even pass an annual budget. They constantly bicker, which means that they just throw all our problems and our huge debt on to our children and possibly our grandchildren.

This has to stop.

Finally, I realized that America doesn't need more "all-talk, no-action" politicians running things. It needs smart business-people who understand how to manage. We don't need more political rhetoric—we need more common sense. "If it ain't broke, don't fix it"—but if it is broke, let's stop talking about it and fix it.

I know how to fix it.

A lot of people were encouraging me to speak out, and I realized that with my well-known success story and record of building residential and office buildings and developing public spaces—all the while accumulating personal wealth—I could inspire people to help create the most massive turnaround in American history.

Of course, there were doubters. Between journalists who sell newspapers by creating controversy, and established politicians eager to preserve the status quo that in turn preserves their jobs, there were many "experts" predicting my demise. They've been reading the "polls." They've been listening to all the lobbyists and special interests saying "Trump is a threat to our well-being." They've even been saying I was a bully or that I was prejudiced or that I hated women or hated Hispanics. Some of them even said—and this is the cardinal sin in politics—I was willing to take on even the richest people in America with all their tax benefits.

I have proven everybody wrong.

EVERYBODY!

Suddenly, those same newspapers and "experts" were only talking about my ideas. And even as I've had to respond to some of the toughest and dumbest questions from supposedly nonpartisan journalists, people continue to listen to me and support my ideas—and guess what? Women are flocking to my message because they're just as tired as men are about how little is being accomplished in Washington.

Likewise, Hispanics are climbing on board because they've heard—from Hispanic employees who've actually worked for me and know me as a boss and leader—that Donald Trump builds businesses.

Donald Trump builds buildings.

Donald Trump develops magnificent golf courses.

Donald Trump makes investments that create jobs.

And Donald Trump creates jobs for legal immigrants and all Americans.

Even the most jaded journalists are realizing that Donald Trump is for real and that the people are responding to someone who is completely different from every other politician.

No one is paying me to say these things. I am paying my own way, and I'm not beholden to any special interests and lobbyists.

I'm not playing by the usual status-quo rules.

I'm not a politician taking polls to see what I should "believe" or be saying.

I am telling it like it is and going to the heart of what I think will make America great again.

I'm not a diplomat who wants everybody else to be happy. I'm a practical businessman who has learned that when you believe in something, you never stop, you never quit, and if you get knocked down, you climb right back up and keep fighting until you win. That's been my strategy all my life, and I've been very successful following it.

Winning matters. Being the best matters.

I'm going to keep fighting for our country until our country is great again.

Too many people think the American dream is dead, but we can bring it back bigger, better, and stronger than ever before. But we must start now.

We need to ensure America starts winning once again.

2

★ ★ ★

OUR "UNBIASED"
POLITICAL MEDIA

FOR A LONG TIME I've been the man the media loves to hate.

It hasn't taken me long to learn how truly dishonest the political media can be. At the first Republican debate, Fox journalist Megyn Kelly was clearly out to get me. And of course, at the second debate, virtually everyone was attacking me because most of their poll numbers were sinking while mine were surging.

I'm perhaps a controversial person. I say what's on my mind. I don't wait to hear what a pollster has to say because I don't use pollsters. The media loves my candor. They know I'm not going to dodge or ignore their questions. I have no problem telling it like it is. These presidential debates would normally have attracted a couple million viewers, but the first night we had 24 million tune in, and the second debate drew a similar number. These were the largest audiences in Fox News' and

CNN's history—bigger than the NBA Finals, the World Series, and most NFL telecasts.

Why do you think people tuned in? To hear the nasty questions? To watch a bunch of politicians trying to pretend they are outsiders (like I truly am) so they can be more successful? The fact is I give people what they need and deserve to hear— exactly what they don't get from politicians—and that is The Truth. Our country is a mess right now and we don't have time to pretend otherwise. We don't have time to waste on being politically correct.

You listen to the politicians and it's as if they are speaking from a script titled "How Boring Can I Possibly Be?" Watching some of these people being interviewed is about as exciting as watching paint dry. They're so afraid of tripping on their own words, terrified that they're going to say something unscripted and go off message—that's the phrase they use, "go off message"—that they are verbally paralyzed. They'll do anything they can to avoid answering a question—and the media plays the game with them.

The object of this game is to appear thoughtful while still looking like a regular guy (or gal) who would be fun to have a beer with. The pollsters tell them how to be everything to everybody without alienating anyone. These same politicians who boldly promise they are going to stand up to our enemies won't even give direct answers to reporters. I don't play that game, because I'm a very successful businessman and my mind-set is that this country needs to bring itself back from the depths of all our problems and the $19 trillion we owe.

At the first debate, I responded to Megyn Kelly's adversarial question by telling her, "I think the big problem this country has is being politically correct. I've been challenged by so many people, and I don't frankly have time for total political correctness. And to be honest with you, this country doesn't have time either. This country is in big trouble. We don't win anymore. We lose to China. We lose to Mexico both in trade and at the border. We lose to Russia and Iran and Saudi Arabia."

I'm not bragging when I say that I'm a winner. I have experience in winning. That's what we call leadership. That means that people will follow me and be inspired by what I do. How do I know? I've been a leader my whole life. Thousands of my employees know that I'll deliver and help them deliver. Sometimes I can be self-effacing, injecting a little humor, having some fun, and kidding around. We have a good time. What I say is what I say, and everyone that knows me really appreciates it.

With the problems we're facing, these debates have become "Trump versus The Others." The attacks are coming at me from all directions, because they all know I am the only one talking about really changing this country and making America great again. The moderators read some quote of mine (or misinterpret a quote of mine) and then ask someone else to comment. Do I have the right temperament? Would I run the country like a business? When did I "actually become a Republican?" These exchanges make great TV. Sadly, they're almost like watching a sporting event.

And guess what? Few, if any, of these questions get to the heart of what is wrong with our country and what really matters to Americans. It's all very personal, because politicians (and their journalist cronies) know that the public doesn't want to hear the details of our nuclear sellout to Iran or what we're going to do about all the federal red ink bleeding the American taxpayer dry these days. The personal exchanges between me and the others become the big story of the debate and the focus of news coverage for weeks. You'd like to think that Fox News and CNN could do better. For the record, I think CNN and Fox treated me badly. Still, you'd think a major news network would take their responsibilities more seriously and use these debates to help the public determine who has the best plan to make our country great again.

But they missed that opportunity.

The whole debate format has worked out fine for me. The American people are smart and figured out pretty quickly what the real motives are for turning up the personal attacks against me. And I get more minutes, more front-page coverage, more requests for interviews than anyone else—and most important for America—the opportunity to speak directly to the people.

There are many reporters whom I have a lot of respect for, especially in the financial media. When the financial journalists interview you they know what they're doing, and they ask direct questions that can provide important information to their viewers. There's money at stake and they don't play the same silly "gotcha" games as the political media do. They can't afford to.

I don't mind being attacked. I use the media the way the media uses me—to attract attention. Once I have that attention, it's up to me to use it to my advantage. I learned a long time ago that if you're not afraid to be outspoken, the media will write about you or beg you to come on their shows. If you do things a little differently, if you say outrageous things and fight back, they love you. So sometimes I make outrageous comments and give them what they want—viewers and readers—in order to make a point. I'm a businessman with a brand to sell. When was the last time you saw a sign hanging outside a pizzeria claiming "The fourth best pizza in the world"?! But now I am using those talents, honed through years of tremendous success, to inspire people to think that our country can get better and be great again and that we can turn things around.

The cost of a full-page ad in the *New York Times* can be more than $100,000. But when they write a story about one of my deals, it doesn't cost me a cent, and I get more important publicity. I have a mutually profitable two-way relationship with the media—we give each other what we need. And now I am using that relationship to talk about the future of America.

Many people believe I do well with the press. Maybe I do, sometimes, but anyone who believes I can use the media is absolutely wrong. Nobody can use the press. It's too big, too widespread. For me, it has been absolutely necessary to try to build relationships with reporters. There are many journalists I respect. Some of the finest people I know are journalists. They are honest, decent, and hardworking; they bring honor to their profession. If I do something wrong or make a mistake, they report it accurately. I've got no problem with that. The mistake bothers me, not the reporting.

But there also are a lot of times I believe that the media is abusive, both to people like me and to the process. The key word is "accurately." Like in every other profession, there are people who are not good. There is no question that considering all the press I've had, both good and bad, I've definitely met people at both the very top as well as the lowest end of the food chain. I mean, the very bottom: They are horrible human beings, they are dishonest. I've seen these so-called journalists flat-out lie. I say that because incompetence doesn't begin to explain the inaccurate stories they have written. There is no other explanation.

The image I created through the media enabled me to build one of the greatest luxury brands in the world. People buy my apartments, buy my label, and play on my golf courses, because they know if I put my name on it, it has to be top quality. Why do you think NBC gave me my own show, *The Apprentice*? They did it because I set myself apart to be a target, the big, tough employer. The result was one of the most successful shows in television history. I'm the only boss in the world who boosts a person's future status by firing them.

Sometimes the truth hurts, but sometimes that is the only way to get better. And a lot of the viewers told me that by watching my show they learned how to be more effective in their jobs so *they* wouldn't get fired.

I don't mind criticism. People call me thin-skinned, but I have thick skin. I have a wonderful and beautiful wife. I've got billions of dollars. My children are highly intelligent and accomplished executives who work with me. I've got a pile of potentially huge projects sitting on my desk. I can't walk into a room or down a street without people racing toward me and telling me that they are excited for our country to win again. So criticism doesn't bother me, and it can't hurt me. I've had power and I've had profits, but now it's time to help the people have a voice and to make sure the people are heard. I am doing this to make our country great again.

Not too long ago, a lot of the pundits kept asking me if I was serious. I thought they were asking the wrong question. What they should have been asking was if I was serious about the future of our country. I have never been more serious about anything in my life.

In the quest for ratings, every show is trying to make news. The problem is that they aren't doing their job. They aren't interested in informing the public. Instead, they play their own game, the "gotcha" game. As I've said, some of the political media are very dishonest. They don't care about printing the truth, they don't want to repeat my entire remarks, and they don't want to be bothered explaining what I meant. They know what I said, they know what I meant, and they edit it or interpret it to have a different meaning.

I was reminded of this behavior when I announced that I was running for president on June 16 in New York. I spoke at great length about a lot of different topics. I listed a lot of the problems we were facing: illegal immigration, underemployment, a shrinking gross domestic product, an aging nuclear arsenal, and Islamic terrorism. I went through them all. What did the media focus on? They concentrated on the fact that I said Mexico was sending its worst people over our southern border. "They're sending people that have lots of problems," I said. "And they're bringing those problems to us."

The next thing you heard was that Trump said all immigrants were criminals. That wasn't what I said at all, but it made a better story for the media. It gave them some headlines. What I said was that among all the illegal immigrants coming from Mexico were some pretty bad people, some of them are rapists, some of them are drug dealers, some of them are coming here to live off the system, and we'd better take immediate and tough measures to close our borders to "illegals."

People who know me know I would never insult Hispanics or any group of people. I've done business with many Hispanics. I've lived in New York all my life. I know how wonderful the Latino culture can be. I know the contributions they make to our country. I've employed many hardworking Hispanic people through the years. I have great respect for Hispanic people, but that's not what the media reported.

Here's what the media reported: TRUMP CALLS ALL IMMIGRANTS CRIMINALS and TRUMP CALLS ALL MEXICANS RAPISTS!

Completely ridiculous.

One of the problems the political media has with me is that I'm not afraid of them. Others run around practically begging for attention. I don't. People respond to my ideas. These media types sell more magazines when my face is on the cover, or when I bring a bigger audience to their television show than they normally attract, and by far. And what's funny is that it turns out the best way for them to get that attention is to criticize me.

But the American people are beginning to understand that. They have finally figured out that a lot of the political media aren't trying to give the people a fair representation of the important issues. Instead, they are trying to manipulate the people—and the election—in favor of the candidates they want to see elected. These media companies are owned by billionaires. These are smart people who know which candidates are going to be best for them, and they find a way to support the person they want.

It would be impossible for me to even estimate how many times I've been interviewed by how many reporters. I couldn't even tell you how many magazine covers I've been on.

Recently, I was interviewed by conservative radio host Hugh Hewitt. "Best interview in America," he called me. Here's what happened:

During the show, he started asking me a series of questions about an Iranian general and various terrorist leaders. "I'm looking for the next commander in chief to know who Hassan Nasrallah is, and Zawahiri, and al-Julani, and al-Baghdadi. Do you know the players without a scorecard yet?"

What a ridiculous question. I don't think knowing the names of each terrorist leader more than a year before the election is a test of whether someone is qualified. We're not playing Trivial Pursuit. Every question Hugh asked me was like that—although I noticed he didn't ask too many questions about our economic policy or about reforming the tax system—things I've spent my life mastering. Instead, he asked these "gotcha" questions that proved nothing except that he was able to read some names and pronounce them correctly. Does anybody believe George W. Bush and Barack Obama could name the leaders of all terrorist organizations? (Not that they are the standard!)

People see through this nonsense. We have real problems and I am talking about how to fix them, and the media continues to play these same old games. In the end though, Hugh Hewittt was just fine, and has since said some great things about me.

Every question was "gotcha, gotcha, gotcha." I gave Hewitt the best possible answer: Those people probably won't even be there in a year. I should have added that if America doesn't do the right things, we won't be help much longer either.

Let me tell you something: When I need to know something, I know it. When I decided to build the most magnificent golf resort in the world in Aberdeen, Scotland, I didn't know the names of the Scottish officials who would be involved in this project—but by the time we went to work, I knew every person it was necessary to know. I'd probably met most of them, too. At the beginning of any kind of project I know what I need to know—and then I get the information to make sure the project gets done to my satisfaction. And I have strong executives who know how to—as their title suggests—execute.

So here's the way I work: I find the people who are the best in the world at what needs to be done, then I hire them to do it, and *then I let them do it* . . . but I always watch over them.

We have great military leaders in this country. We produce the finest officers and soldiers anywhere in the world. And we have some really smart men and women working in our intelligence community. These people spend all day, every day, working on serious problems. These professionals are the real experts. They know all the players.

One reason that I have been successful in business is that I hire the best people. I pay them well, and I keep them working for me. There are times when I meet someone working on the other side of the deal. Maybe they don't beat me, but they give me a tough time. I respect that. In fact, I respect that so much that sometimes I hire them away from the company they were negotiating for.

Truthfully though, I can't really blame Hugh Hewitt for doing what he did. Just like Megyn Kelly, he figured out that the best way to get attention is to attack Donald Trump. This guy got more headlines from our little exchange than he probably ever got in his whole career. It wasn't the names of terrorist leaders that he cared about—it was his own name. And it worked for him.

It's just the same old game, where the people come last. That needs to change, too.

Begging for attention really sums up the problem we face in this country with our media. There is such competition that they're more interested in entertaining their audience than educating them. They like me because I help them attract more viewers. They hate me because they know I don't need them. I learned a long time ago how to talk directly to the people who matter—to regular Americans who are fed up with the career politicians.

That's probably you—the real Americans—which is why I've written this book.

3

★ ★ ★

IMMIGRATION: GOOD WALLS
MAKE GOOD NEIGHBORS

WHEN I ANNOUNCED MY candidacy I spoke for almost an hour, covering just about every challenge that we're facing. But the subject that got the most attention was my focus on our immigration policy. Or, in fact, our lack of any coherent immigration policy. I was pretty tough on illegal immigrants, and a lot of people didn't like that. I said that many countries are dumping their worst people on our border and that it has to stop. A country that doesn't control its borders can't survive—especially with what's going on right now.

What I said only makes common sense. I speak to border patrol guards, and they tell us who we're letting across our border. The countries south of us are not sending us their best people. The bad people are coming from places other than just Mexico. They're coming from all over Central and South

America, and they're coming probably—probably—from the Middle East. Let me add now: Allowing tens of thousands of Syrian refugees in the door will certainly bring a lot of problems. But we won't know how bad, because we have no protection and we have no competence. We don't know what's happening. It's got to stop, and it's got to stop quickly.

Later in my announcement I added, "I would build a great wall, and nobody builds walls better than me, believe me, and I'll build it very inexpensively. I will build a great wall on our southern border. And I will have Mexico pay for that wall. Mark my words." I spoke for quite a while that day. I covered just about all the problems our country is facing. But what did the media report about that speech? "Trump is anti-immigration." "Trump calls immigrants rapists." "Trump is starting a war with Mexico." You want to know why we aren't solving our problems? Why nothing changes? It's because we're not facing the problems and taking action.

The flow of illegal immigrants into this country is one of the most serious problems we face. It's killing us. But until I made that point during my speech, nobody was talking about it honestly. And instead of saying, "Trump's right and we'd better do something to stop illegal immigration right now or we're going to lose our country," they said, "Oh, what a terrible thing Trump said about the nice people who live south of our borders. I hope they don't get upset at us because of that. Maybe he'll apologize." I understand why that happened. It's a lot easier to criticize me for being blunt than it is to actually admit this immigration situation is a dangerous problem and then to find a way to deal with it.

Let me state this clearly: *I am not against immigration.*

My mother emigrated to this country from Scotland in 1918 and married my father, whose parents had come here from Germany in 1885. My parents were two of the best people who ever lived, and it was millions of people like them who made this country so wonderful and so successful.

I love immigration.

Immigrants come to this country, they want to work hard, be successful, raise their kids, and share in the American dream. It's a beautiful story. I can close my eyes and just imagine what my relatives must have been thinking when they sailed past the Statue of Liberty into New York and their new lives. And if they could only see the results of their risk and sacrifice! How can anyone not appreciate the courage it took for these people to leave their families and come here?

What I don't love is the concept of illegal immigration.

It's not fair to everyone else, including people who have been waiting on line for years to come into our country legally. And the flood of illegal immigrants coming across our borders has become a dangerous problem. We don't protect our borders. We don't know who's here, but I bet wherever they came from knows that they are gone. Yet those governments do nothing to help us. The estimate is that there are 11 million illegal immigrants in America, but the fact is that nobody knows how many there really are. We have no way of tracking them.

What we do know is that some of those immigrants are a source of real crime. In 2011, the Government Accountability Office reported that there were three million arrests that could be attributed to the incarcerated alien population, including tens of thousands of violent criminals. There were 351,000 criminal illegal aliens in our prisons—that number does not include the crime of crossing our borders. It costs us more than a billion dollars a year just to keep these people in prison.

I understand that the vast majority of these people are honest, decent, hardworking people who came here to improve their own lives and their children's lives. America holds so much promise, and what honest person wouldn't want to come here to try to make a better life for himself and his children? But illegal immigration is a problem that must be confronted by the United States government who, in turn, must confront other countries. I feel as sorry for these individuals as anyone else does. Conditions in some of their countries are deplorable.

Nonetheless, illegal immigration has to stop. A country that can't protect its borders isn't a country. We are the only country in the world whose immigration system places the needs of other nations ahead of our own.

There is a word to describe people who do that: fools.

I have great respect for the people of Mexico. The people have tremendous spirit. I've been involved in deals with Mexican businessmen. But those businessmen aren't the people the Mexican government is sending us. Too many people have forgotten the Mariel boatlift. In 1980, Fidel Castro told the Cuban people that anyone who wanted to leave Cuba was free to do so. President Carter opened our borders to anyone who came here. Except Castro was too smart for him. He emptied Cuba's prisons and insane asylums and sent his biggest problems here. He got rid of the worst people in that country, and we were left to deal with them. More than 125,000 Cubans came here, and despite there being many, many great ones, some were criminals or had mental problems. More than thirty years later we're still dealing with that.

Does anybody really believe that the Mexican government—for that matter, all the governments in South and Central America—didn't get that message? The Mexican government has published pamphlets explaining how to illegally emigrate to the United States. Which makes my point—this is not about a few individuals seeking a better life; this is about foreign governments behaving badly and our own career politicians and "leaders" not doing their jobs.

And who can blame these foreign governments? It's a great way for those governments to get rid of their worst people without paying any price for their bad behavior. Instead of putting these bad people in their prisons, they send them to us. And the bad guys are bringing the drug business and other criminal activity with them. Some of them are rapists, as a matter of fact, and as we have now seen in San Francisco, some of them are killers. The man who shot and killed a beautiful young woman had been pushed out of Mexico five times. He should have been in jail there, but instead they sent him here.

The price we're paying for illegal immigration is enormous.

It has to stop.

The first thing we need to do is secure our southern border—and we need to do it now. We have to stop that flood, and the best way to do that is to build a wall. People say you can't do it—how do you build a wall across the whole border?

Believe me, it can be done.

Nobody can build a wall like me. I will build a great wall on our southern border. It doesn't have to cover the entire border. Some areas are already secured with physical barriers. In other areas the terrain is too difficult for people to cross. It's probably about 1,000 miles we will need to secure with the new wall.

There are people who say it can't be done, that it's not possible to build a wall 1,000 miles long. Except beginning more than 2,000 years ago the Chinese built a wall that eventually stretched almost 13,000 miles that could never be breached. It was a combination of massive walls, impassible trenches and ditches, and rugged natural terrain, as well as an estimated 25,000 watchtowers. Believe me, our wall-building technology has improved a lot in 2,000 years. What we don't have that the Chinese had is the commitment to do it. They understood the danger of leaving their border unprotected and they did something about it. We talk about it and do nothing.

Walls work. The Israelis spent $2 million per kilometer to build a wall—which has been hugely successful in stopping terrorists from getting into the country. Ironically, some of the same people who claim we shouldn't build this wall cite the success of Israel's wall. While obviously we don't face the same level of terrorist threat as our closest Middle East ally, there is no question about the value of a wall in the fight against terrorism.

Many people don't know that even Mexico has built its own wall on its southern border—to keep out illegal immigrants.

It wouldn't even be that difficult. We already have a model: Yuma, Arizona, for example, built three walls separated by a 75-yard no-man's-land that allows border agents to patrol within that area with their vehicles. They installed cameras, radio communications, radar, and a great lighting system. After it was built, the 120-mile-long stretch known as the Yuma sector saw an incredible 72 percent decrease in the number of people apprehended trying to get into this country illegally—and mine will be much better.

Construction of the wall needs to start as soon as possible. And Mexico has to pay for it.

Let me repeat that, one way or another: Mexico will pay for it.

How? We could increase the various border fees we charge. We could increase the fees on temporary visas. We could even impound remittance payments derived from illegal wages. Foreign governments could tell their embassies to start helping, otherwise they risk troubled relations with America.

If necessary we could pay for the wall through a tariff or cut foreign aid to Mexico or simply make it clear to the Mexican government that it is to the benefit of their very profitable—for them—relationship with the United States to pay for it.

But one way or another, they are going to pay for it.

I don't mind putting a big, beautiful door in that wall so people can come in and out . . . LEGALLY.

The wall will be a good start, but by itself it won't be enough. Without the wall, however, everything else is more of the same old big talk we hear from the politicians.

We've been trying to get this problem under control for more than 75 years. We've tried a lot of different solutions, and the result is that now illegal immigration is worse than ever. One of the solutions that did show promise was President Eisenhower's attempt to deal with illegal immigration on our southern border, which had become known as the truly terribly named "Operation Wetback." But even with that awful name the program was successful. It was a joint effort between the INS and the Mexican government. Special immigration teams were created to quickly process and deport illegal immigrants. One of the reasons it worked is that people who were caught were given to Mexican government agents, who moved them into central Mexico, where they could find jobs. In the first year, more than one million people were sent back.

What we need is the comprehensive program I have outlined that will enable us to get our immigration system under control. It starts with enforcing the existing laws. A country either has laws or it doesn't. But having laws that we don't enforce makes no sense to me. And in addition to keeping bad people from coming in, we've got to get the criminals out. When you break our laws you get thrown out. It's simple. Why should we absorb the expense of keeping criminals in prisons? Let their countries of origin deal with the problems they sent us. If they refuse to take them back, we can stop issuing visas to those countries, preventing their citizens from legally visiting the United States.

I also would triple the number of immigration officers we currently employ until the wall is built. We are asking these people to do a job that would be difficult even if they had all the support they need, and they don't. Think of it this way: Currently there are about 5,000 officers attempting to enforce the existing immigration laws against the more than 11 million illegal aliens. Compare that to the 10,000 members of the Los Angeles Police Department or the 35,000 officers in the New York Police Department. Since 9/11 we have tripled the size of the border patrol but haven't substantially increased the number of ICE officers—the officers who enforce immigration laws.

The career politicians love to talk about having a nationwide "E-verify system" so potential employers will be able to determine who is here legally and eligible for work and who isn't. Certainly, this will help protect the jobs for unemployed Americans. But let's not kid ourselves. Our "leaders" must lead on this, and engage with foreign governments to stop illegal immigration, and not simply impose something on our businesses and think that some Internet verification system alone will solve the problem.

We have to cut off federal grants to sanctuary cities—those places that refuse to cooperate with federal law enforcement and actually abet criminal behavior—we have to end them. I repeat, we either are a nation of laws or we're not.

We also need to do what is necessary to enforce our visa regulations. People get a visa and come here legally, and when that visa expires, many stay here illegally. If they get caught, nothing happens to them. That's got to change. We need to have real penalties for people who overstay their visas. I am sick and tired of hearing politicians who are all talk and no action. President Obama and his people are great at sending letters and press releases, but they never seem to have any consequences for foreign governments that don't listen to them.

Most important is ending or curtailing so-called birthright citizenship, or anchor babies. American citizenship is an extraordinary gift. Its value over a lifetime can't be measured. So the fact that the Fourteenth Amendment has been interpreted to mean that any child born in the United States automatically is an American citizen—and that baby can be used as an anchor to keep its family here—is the single biggest magnet attracting illegal immigrants.

The Fourteenth Amendment was never intended to be used that way. The original purpose of the Fourteenth Amendment, which was ratified in 1868, following the Civil War, was to guarantee all rights granted to citizens in the Constitution to freed slaves. No serious historian could possibly interpret any of the supporting language in the Congressional Record that the birthright citizenship was intended for anyone other than the freed slaves.

It wasn't until 1898 that the Supreme Court ruled that, with certain specific exceptions, the provisions of the Fourteenth Amendment granted citizenship to the children of those lawfully here who gave birth on American soil. By a huge margin, Americans want to change that policy. Even Democrat Harry Reid admitted that "no sane country" would grant citizenship to the children of illegal immigrants. It's estimated that about 300,000 of these children are born here annually. That's 300,000 children who are entitled to all the rights and privileges granted to American citizens because their mothers entered this country illegally by walking over the border for a day in the south or by flying in from another country under fraudulent documentation. There are businesses that specialize in making this happen! They call it "birth tourism"—pregnant foreign women travel to this country just so that they can give birth here to babies who then automatically become American citizens.

Citizenship is not a gift we can afford to keep giving away, and I will find a legal way of stopping this policy. A lot of really smart people and lawyers believe the Fourteenth Amendment was never intended to create a whole new path to citizenship. We're going to test it every possible way. We will win in court and we will win in Congress.

I don't want to stop legal immigration to this country. In fact, I would like to reform and increase immigration in some important ways. Our current immigration laws are upside down—they make it tough on the people we need to have here, and easy for the people we don't want here.

This country is a magnet for many of the smartest, hardest-working people born in other countries, yet we make it difficult for these bright people who follow the laws to settle here.

It's amazing that people who come here to earn a master's degree and who demonstrate wonderful skills are forced to wait on a very long line when they want to stay and contribute to this country. In fact, for a lot of them, their number may never be called. Bright young kids come here from all over the world to study in our colleges. They get the best education in the world. They graduate with honors and we hand them a diploma and a plane ticket. Their mistake is that they are honest people—they follow the law. They want to stay here, but we send them back to their countries, and ultimately they use the knowledge they gained here to compete against us.

If you're a criminal, though, or an unskilled worker, or someone escaping criminal charges in another country, you are able to sneak into our country and in many cases get some benefits and never leave. These "enforcement" policies and this backward approach to immigration have to change. Our immigration policy needs to work to make America great again.

My immigration policy is actually pretty simple. We need to make changes to our laws to make it easier for those people who can contribute to this country to come here legally while making it impossible for criminal elements and other people to get here illegally. I want good people to come here from all over the world, but I want them to do so legally. We can expedite the process, we can reward achievement and excellence, but we have to respect the legal process. And those people who take advantage of the system and come here illegally should never enjoy the benefits of being a resident—or citizen—of this nation. So I am against any path to citizenship for undocumented workers or anyone else who is in this country illegally.

They should—and need to—go home and get in line.

And you know who agrees with me? The Mexicans, the Chinese, and all the people from other countries who want to be here legally and can't get a visa or fit into a quota, yet see millions of people living here illegally. They don't understand how we can undermine our own interests.

If you have laws that you don't enforce, then you don't have laws. This leads to lawlessness.

We can be generous and do all of this humanely. But the security and prosperity of American citizens have to come first.

Our country, our people, and our laws have to be our top priority.

4

* ★ ★ ★

FOREIGN POLICY:
FIGHTING FOR PEACE

THE CAREER DIPLOMATS WHO got us into many foreign policy messes say I have no experience in foreign policy. They think that successful diplomacy requires years of experience and an understanding of all the nuances that have to be carefully considered before reaching a conclusion. Only then do these pin-striped bureaucrats *consider* taking action.

Look at the state of the world right now. It's a terrible mess, and that's putting it kindly.

There has never been a more dangerous time. The so-called insiders within the Washington ruling class are the people who got us into this trouble. So why should we continue to pay attention to them?

Some of these so-called "experts" are trying to scare people by saying that my approach would make the world more dangerous.

More dangerous? More dangerous than *what*? More dangerous than where we are now?

Here's what I know—what we are doing now isn't working.
And years ago, when I was just starting out in business, I figured
out a pretty simple approach that has always worked well for me:

*When you're digging yourself deeper and deeper into a hole,
stop digging.*

My approach to foreign policy is built on a strong foundation: Operate from strength. That means we have to maintain
the strongest military in the world, by far. We have to demonstrate a willingness to use our economic strength to reward
those countries that work with us and punish those countries
that don't. That means going after the banks and financial in-
stitutions that launder money for our enemies, then move it
around to facilitate terrorism. And we have to create alliances
with our allies that reveal mutual benefits.

If we're going to continue to be the policemen of the world,
we ought to be paid for it.

Teddy Roosevelt always believed we should "speak softly
and carry a big stick." I've never been afraid to speak up to
protect my interests and, truthfully, I don't understand why we
don't speak more loudly about the ways we are losing around
the world. If we don't speak up, how is anything ever going to
get better? How are we ever going to win?

America is the most powerful country in the world and we
shouldn't be afraid to say it. "Iron Mike" Tyson, the famous
fighter, once explained his philosophy, saying, "Everybody has
a plan until they get punched in the mouth."

The first thing we need to do is build up our ability to

throw that punch. We need to spend whatever it takes to completely fund our military properly. Fifteen years ago I wrote, "We can't pursue forward military and foreign-policy objectives on a backward military budget."

The best way *not* to have to use your military power is to make sure that power is visible.

When people know that we will use force if necessary and that we really mean it, we'll be treated differently.

With respect.

Right now, no one believes us because we've been so weak with our approach to military policy in the Middle East and elsewhere.

Building up our military is cheap when you consider the alternative. We're buying peace and we're locking in our national security. Right now we are in bad shape militarily. We're decreasing the size of our forces and we're not giving them the best equipment. Recruiting the best people has fallen off, and we can't get the people we have trained to the level they need to be. There are a lot of questions about the state of our nuclear weapons. When I read reports of what is going on, I'm shocked.

It's no wonder nobody respects us. It's no surprise that we never win.

Spending money on our military is also smart business. Who do people think build our airplanes and ships, and all the equipment that our troops should have? American workers, that's who. So building up our military also makes economic sense because it allows us to put real money into the system and put thousands of people back to work.

There is another way to pay to modernize our military forces. If other countries are depending on us to protect them, shouldn't they be willing to make sure we have the capability to do it? Shouldn't they be willing to pay for the servicemen and servicewomen and the equipment we're providing?

Depending on the price of oil, Saudi Arabia earns somewhere between half a billion and a billion dollars every day. They wouldn't exist, let alone have that wealth, without our protection. We get nothing from them. Nothing.

We defend Germany. We defend Japan. We defend South Korea. These are powerful and wealthy countries. We get nothing from them.

It's time to change all that. It's time to win again.

We've got 28,500 wonderful American soldiers on South Korea's border with North Korea. They're in harm's way every single day. They're the only thing that is protecting South Korea. And what do we get from South Korea for it? They sell us products—at a nice profit. They compete with us.

We spent two trillion dollars doing whatever we did in Iraq. I still don't know why we did it, but we did. Iraq is sitting on an ocean of oil. Is it out of line to suggest that they should contribute to their own future? And after the blood and the money we spent trying to bring some semblance of stability to the Iraqi people, maybe they should be willing to make sure we can rebuild the army that fought for them.

When Kuwait was attacked by Saddam Hussein, all the wealthy Kuwaitis ran to Paris. They didn't just rent suites—they took up whole buildings, entire hotels. They lived like kings while their country was occupied.

Who did they turn to for help? Who else? Uncle Sucker. That's us.

We spent billions of dollars sending our army to win back Kuwait. Our people were killed and wounded, but the Iraqis went back to their country.

About two months after the war, several Kuwaitis came up to my office to discuss a deal I wanted to do with them. Believe me, they would not have lost money on this deal. They told me, "No, no, no, we do not like the United States for investment purposes. We have great respect for you, but we want to invest outside of the United States."

We had just handed them back their country!

They were watching TV in the best hotel rooms in Paris while our kids were fighting for them. And they didn't want to invest in this country?

How stupid are we?!

Why didn't the United States make a deal with them that outlined how they would pay for us to get their country back for them? They would have paid anything if just asked.

The point is, we're spending trillions of dollars to safeguard other countries. We're paying for the privilege of fighting their battles. It makes no sense to me.

It really is time the rest of the world paid their fair share, and if I have anything to say about it, they will!

★

The biggest question people ask about foreign policy is at what point do we put boots on the ground? We can't be afraid to use our military, but sending our sons and daughters should be the very last resort. I've seen what wars do to our kids. I've seen their broken bodies, know all about the horrors that live in their heads, and the enormous effects of trauma. We cannot commit American troops to battle without a real and tangible objective.

My rules of engagement have always been pretty simple—if we are going to intervene in a conflict, there had better be a direct threat to our national interests. The threat should be so obvious that most Americans will know where the hot spot is on the globe and will quickly understand why we are getting involved. Also, we'd better have an airtight plan to win and get out.

In other words, my strategy would be the exact opposite of our strategy in going to war with Iraq.

Iraq was no threat to us. The American people had no idea why the Bush administration decided to attack.

Our brilliant strategists had to twist our intelligence reports and drum up reasons for an invasion. We targeted Saddam Hussein's alleged weapons of mass destruction as a justification. There was no plan (or a very flawed one) to win and leave. Before the war started I came out very strongly against it. It made no sense to me. I said then that it would be a disaster and would destabilize the Middle East. I said that without Iraq to hold them back, Iran would attempt to take over the Middle East.

And that's exactly what has happened.

There are some places in the world where massive force is necessary. The threat from ISIS is real. It is a new kind of enemy and it has to be stopped. The longer we wait before doing that, the more dangerous it will become. We don't need another 9/11 to understand that these people want to kill us, and we're not doing enough to prevent them from spreading their vicious brand of terrorism. The headlines and videos tell us what we're dealing with: rapes, kidnapping, and lining up civilians in order to cut their heads off. There is also strong evidence that ISIS is resorting to chemical warfare.

It's time to get serious about our response. Either we're fighting to win or we're going to continue to be big losers.

Unfortunately, it may require boots on the ground to fight the Islamic State. I don't think it's necessary to broadcast our strategy. (In fact, one of the most ridiculous policy blunders President Obama has committed was to announce our timetable for withdrawal from Iraq and Afghanistan.) If military advisers recommend it, we should commit a limited—but sufficient—number of troops to fight on the ground. We could also easily expand air operations to make it impossible for ISIS to ever find safe haven anywhere in the region. Our policy of trying to be "advisers" in the field has certainly been a failure.

However, I have a unique perspective on what action we should take. While ISIS is our most violent enemy, they ended up with oil in Iraq and Syria that we should have taken. That oil, along with ransom and extortion, is funding their army. I've advocated bombing the hell out of those oil fields to cut off the source of their money. This would barely affect the world oil supply, but it would dramatically reduce their ability to fund terrorism.

We have to take that oil because it is the source of their wealth. We would hit them so hard and so fast in so many different ways they wouldn't know what happened. And then we'd hit them again and again until ISIS ceased to exist as a threat to anybody.

We don't have a choice. These people are medieval barbarians. They cut off heads, they drown people, they torture people, and we can't allow them to ever gain a safe foothold anywhere.

The number of ISIS troops is relatively small. Our intelligence community has estimated that there are no more than 30,000 to 50,000 ISIS fighters. People are usually surprised by that number. ISIS has done such a good job promoting fear that people assume it to be a much larger force. It isn't. The entire ISIS force probably wouldn't even fill Yankee Stadium. So defeating them requires a real commitment to go after them relentlessly wherever they are, without stopping, until every one of them is dead—and always bringing in other countries to help out.

Iran is a much more complex problem.

I am not afraid to criticize President Obama when he gets it wrong. When he was running for president in 2008, he correctly said, "Iran is a grave threat. It has an illicit nuclear program, it supports terrorism across the region and militias in Iraq, it threatens Israel's existence, and it denies the Holocaust."

So why when Iran was struggling financially would he agree to a nuclear deal that releases billions of dollars' worth of assets, which will further subsidize their terrorism business? It makes no sense.

Iran was a powerful nation until the religious fanatics took over. As long as those people remain in power, Iran will be our enemy and a threat to Israel's existence. Their supreme leader, Ayatollah Khamenei, has promised that Israel won't exist in 25 years. We have to take that threat seriously and act accordingly.

I've always loved and admired the Jewish people and supported the special relationship we have with Israel. The next president has to restore our traditionally strong partnership. We have been there for Israel and will continue to be there for Israel, because it is the one stable democracy in that region. It has become a fair-trading partner and a fellow pioneer on the frontiers of medicine, communications, technology, and energy development, which will benefit both of our nations well into the future.

The miles that separate us right now from Iran are only a temporary barrier for them. If, or when, they develop missiles that can reach this country they will become a much greater threat. Meanwhile, they are financially supporting terrorist groups all over the world—and those groups are a real threat to our country and to our military serving overseas. Our enemies no longer need huge armies or billion-dollar missile systems to attack this country. Technology has made it possible for one or two terrorists to inflict terrible damage on us. We've got to stop Iran from sponsoring these murderers.

But instead, we continue losing.

The deal President Obama negotiated with Iran was the worst I have ever seen. We couldn't have done worse.

Iran was boxed in and the sanctions were hurting them. President Obama put his "legacy" on the line and before we walked into negotiations, the mullahs knew he had to have a deal or end up looking even more incompetent, so they fleeced him.

Disgraceful.

We did everything wrong in those negotiations. Instead of removing the sanctions that forced the Iranians to negotiate, we should have doubled or tripled the sanctions.

Remember the principal strategy of negotiation: *The side*

that needs the deal the most is the one that should walk away with the least.

I would have increased the sanctions until the conditions there were so terrible that the Iranian leaders were begging for a deal.

I would have laid down certain conditions that had to be agreed to, starting with the release of our four prisoners.

I wouldn't have settled for less than a complete dismantling of all their nuclear facilities, destruction of all their centrifuges, and on-site inspections anytime, anywhere.

We didn't get any of that—none of it—and then we released billions of dollars that had been frozen.

We literally paid them to force us to accept a terrible deal. That would be like me beginning negotiations to build another magnificent skyscraper along the Hudson with 50-mile views in all directions, and walking out with approval to put up a small three-story building facing a wall.

Iran got what it wanted (the release of their seized assets) and in return gave up what might have seemed like huge concessions, only to find out that there were so many loopholes that it will be nearly impossible to enforce anything meaningful.

The possibility of Iran defying the world and developing a nuclear weapon is still very real. If the Iranians decide to prevent us (or the International Atomic Energy Agency) from inspecting their facilities, there isn't too much that we can do about it other than take military action. The coalition of countries that enforced those sanctions is finished. Those countries—and several of them couldn't care less about

Israel—had people in Tehran talking business before the ink had dried on the side agreements.

And then President Obama wouldn't let Congress look at the deal. Once the new Iranian "partners" start making money there is no way the sanctions can ever be put back into place.

Unfortunately, the deal is done. Once the sanctions are removed there is no going back, no "snapback." Putting sanctions back in place unilaterally won't do any good. I am especially good at reading a contract. There is always a loophole, we need to find it and, if necessary, they will pay big-league dollars.

Whatever it takes, whatever we have to do, Iran cannot be allowed to build a nuclear weapon.

There are many different ways to make sure that Iran is never armed with nuclear weapons. I'd be happy to sit down with the Iranian leaders when they understand that the best course for them, if they want to be a major player in the civilized world, is to close down their entire nuclear program. An Iran with a nuclear weapon would start a nuclear arms race in the Middle East with potentially devastating consequences. The situation would rapidly escalate to being the most dangerous threat Israel has ever faced. And it would force us to use extreme measures in defense of Israel and other allies in the region.

That's not going to happen, whatever Iran might think right now.

★

Today the world has to deal with two "sets" of China.

The good China is the one that has built great cities and

provided housing and education for millions of people. The good China allows its citizens to travel around the world and get an education, and has helped create a growing middle class.

The bad China is the one that's mostly hidden to outsiders. It's the government that controls Internet access for its citizens, cracks down on political dissent, closes newspapers, jails dissidents, restricts individual freedoms, launches cyber-attacks, and uses its clout around the world to manipulate economies.

And all the while it is building up its military strength.

There is no question that dealing with China, along with Russia, is going to continue to be our biggest challenge long-term.

Our competition with China right now is economic, and we've been losing that battle for a long time. China has become our third-largest trading partner, behind only our neighbors Canada and Mexico. Yet China holds more of our American debt—more than $1.5 trillion—than any other country. (Although Japan is close.) As we saw in the summer of 2015 when the Chinese stock markets collapsed, our economies are tied together in a very negative way.

Many years ago, there was an adage that "When General Motors sneezes, the stock market catches a cold." In those days, GM was such a big player in the economy that if it stumbled, our economy suffered, too. The recent precipitous decline of the Chinese stock market caused our own Dow Jones average to plummet 1,000 points in a couple of days as investors ran for cover. Likewise, our trade deficit has been a dangerous drag on our economy. When China devalues its currency, this upsets the already tenuous balance of trade.

We know that we have become dependent on the emerging Chinese markets—but they have become dependent on us, too. In 2014, we imported 17 percent more Chinese goods than any other country in the world. Hong Kong, which is a wholly owned subsidiary of China, was second and Japan a distant third. The health of the Chinese economy depends on us. They need our trade more than we need them.

Foolishly, we don't use that to our advantage.

For the last few decades, China's economy has been growing at a phenomenal 9 to 10 percent each year, although more recently there are signs of a cooling off. Despite these recent upheavals, economists have made predictions that within the next decade, China will replace the United States as the world's largest economy. What have we done to make sure we will be able to compete with them? What have we done to beat them?

I'll tell you what we've done: We've rolled over.

There are people who wish I wouldn't refer to China as our enemy. But that's exactly what they are. They have destroyed entire industries by utilizing low-wage workers, cost us tens of thousands of jobs, spied on our businesses, stolen our technology, and have manipulated and devalued their currency, which makes importing our goods more expensive—and sometimes, impossible.

I know from my own experience that this is a difficult problem. The Chinese are very savvy businesspeople, and they have great advantages over our manufacturers. I've had several Trump-brand products made there.

That's a good example of the difference between a politician and a businessman. To stay in business I have to be smarter than my competition. I could make a very important point if I refused to have my goods manufactured there.

As long as we're playing under these conditions American companies don't have a choice. Third-world countries have substantially lower production costs. They have lower overhead and pay their workers a lot less. As a businessman, I have an obligation to all of my employees and to consumers and stockholders to produce the best product at the lowest possible price.

However, as a matter of American global policy, we want to take away China's advantages. Last year, President Obama went to China and they held a beautiful banquet for him. Before Chinese president Xi Jinping made a reciprocal visit here, the White House announced plans for a lavish dinner. I made the point that hosting a state dinner in his honor was about the last thing I would do. Instead I'd tell him it was time we got down to business, and we would go to work. For starters, the Chinese regime must stop devaluing their currency because doing so makes it even harder for the rest of the world to compete.

The reality is that China needs a strong American economy as much as we need their business. In May 2015, for example, Americans bought $1 out of every $5 worth of products China exported that month. We buy almost 20 percent of all their exports, considerably more than the EU does, which is the second-biggest consumer of Chinese goods. And that American percentage is increasing every year, making China more and more dependent on the American consumer for its own prosperity.

As Steve Forbes wrote in his magazine, "China's holdings in US Treasuries, which reached record levels in 2013, are setting off alarm bells. They shouldn't. They underscore that Beijing is becoming more dependent on the US and the rest of the world for its strength and prosperity."

Remember: *The Chinese need us as much as we need them.* Maybe even more.

So what should we do about it? We are going to use the leverage we have to change the situation so that it favors America and our people. We have to start by getting tough with the Chinese. I've negotiated with Chinese companies. I know how they do business. I'm actually landlord to China's largest bank, which has its offices in Trump Tower. We've successfully negotiated several leases. It hasn't always been easy. These are skilled people but I never backed down.

Believe me, I know the best negotiators in this country, and a lot of them would be ready to go to work creating a fair balance of trade. If people like Carl Icahn were representing America, we would see a big difference in our trading policy.

We actually hold a very strong hand. Unfortunately, our politicians are either too stupid or too foolish to understand this. Maybe they are both. We have several very good options, but it is always important to be flexible—and never reveal our cards. Our politicians talk too much.

President Obama makes strong statements and promises us vigorous actions then nothing happens.

So what happens when he makes those promises and never follows through? He loses all his credibility. I wonder what our great generals, men like MacArthur and Patton, would say if they heard a president revealing our plans for the Middle East or daring our enemies to cross a line.

A very good story recently quoted a businessman describing

me as "unpredictable," noting it was one of my better qualities and helped me make a lot of money. Now that I am running for president, which so many experts predicted I would not do, that same trait has made it really hard for all my critics to figure out how to compete with my message. They're all busy playing nicely, following all the establishment rules, taking every predictable step, trying to fit inside the conventional wisdom—and when I don't play that game, they don't know how to respond.

Tipping your hand is one of the dumbest mistakes you can make in a military confrontation. I've read a lot of history and I don't recall reading that General George Washington made hotel reservations in Valley Forge, or that he sent ahead his best wishes to the Hessians in Trenton. The element of surprise wins battles. So I don't tell the other side what I'm doing, I don't warn them, and I don't let them fit me comfortably into a predictable pattern. I don't want people to know exactly what I'm doing—or thinking. I like being unpredictable.

It keeps them off balance.

As a leader, I also know there are times when you should keep your cards close to the vest. When I was assembling property to build a skyscraper, for example, I had to buy many small lots so I could combine them into one very large and valuable buildable location, and total secrecy was an absolute necessity. If the owners of those properties had found out what I was doing they would have been able to squeeze considerably more money out of me for their properties.

My point is that right now we're doing too much talking.

When dealing with China we need to stand up to them and remind them that it's bad business to take advantage of your best customer. And then we should sit down and figure out how to make this a more equitable relationship.

There is no one-size-fits-all foreign policy. We need to make our beliefs very clear and let them form the framework of our policy.

Everything begins with a strong military. Everything.

We will have the strongest military in our history, and our people will be equipped with the best weaponry and protection available.

Period.

That means the best missile systems, the best cyber-warfare training and equipment, and the best-trained soldiers. And when they come home after a war, battered and bruised, our troops won't have to wait months for treatment.

We owe those who serve us the best and the fastest care. It's ridiculous how long our vets have to wait to get the help they deserve. They are our heroes, and the present administration has forgotten them.

So how do we turn the tide and start winning again?

As I've said, it starts with the most advanced and muscular military in the world, the most mobile one as well. We need to put some of the bill for this transformation on the Saudi Arabians, the South Koreans, the Germans, the Japanese, and the British. We're protecting them, after all, and they should share in the costs.

Next, we need to operate from a position of economic

strength. We have the most powerful consumer engine in the world. We just need to start using it to our full advantage.

Nobody likes to do business more than I do, but every deal I make will have one objective: America wins.

We need to use the economic strength of American markets and the American consumer to assist our friends and remind our enemies about the benefits of cooperation.

We need to use those strengths to form stronger alliances with our natural allies, but we need to expect them to be there when they are needed. I still don't understand why Germany and other countries watched impassively as Putin marched into Ukraine. You can be sure Israel can be counted on to stand tall with us in the Middle East.

And finally, we need to pay special attention to the Chinese. Their days of undercutting us with protectionist policies and cyber-theft are over.

The new dawn of America has just begun.

5

*   *   *

EDUCATION: A FAILING GRADE

MY FATHER DID NOT graduate from college. He was too busy working and building his business, but he understood and appreciated the value of an education. He had great respect for people with college degrees, even though he had built a large real estate business and earned many times more than most of them. With my father's financial assistance, his younger brother, John, earned his master's degree in physics from Columbia and his PhD from the Massachusetts Institute of Technology, one of the most prestigious universities in America. John became a noted professor at MIT and invented one of the first million-volt X-ray generators that was used to save the lives of cancer patients. During World War II, he played an important role in the development of radar. President Truman awarded him the President's Certificate of Merit, and he was a recipient of the National Medal of Science.

From my father and my uncle I learned the value of work and the value of a good education. From my own experience I learned what happens when you put them together. I went to the Wharton School of Finance at the University of Pennsylvania, which is, in my opinion, the best business school in America—and arguably the hardest there is to get into.

There is one thing I know that even the professional politicians will support—education is good. It's the easiest statement for a politician to support. But the question is, how do we make sure the best education possible is available for the most American kids?

Because right now that is not the situation.

Like so many other areas that our so-called leaders have wreaked their havoc upon, the American educational system is failing. We're 26th in the world—26th! That's an embarrassment. We spend more money on education, per capita, than any other nation—but 25 countries in the developed world provide a better education for their kids than we do for ours. This is simply unacceptable.

Part of the problem is the politicians! They are unable to run a national education system with a top-down, one-size-fits-all approach. Our states and local districts are doing just fine making their own decisions on how best to educate our children. Now the federal Department of Education has been dictating educational policy for too long, and that needs to stop. Common Core doesn't work.

A lot of people believe the Department of Education should just be eliminated. Get rid of it. If we don't eliminate it completely, we certainly need to cut its power and reach. Education has to be run locally. Common Core, No Child Left Behind, and Race to the Top are all programs that take decisions away from parents and local school boards. These programs allow the progressives in the Department of Education to indoctrinate, not educate, our kids. What they are doing does not fit the American model of governance.

I am totally against these programs and the Department of Education. It's a disaster. We cannot continue to fail our children—the very future of this nation.

I went to a military school, New York Military Academy. It was a tough, tough place. There were ex-drill sergeants all over the place. and these people liked to scream and, above all, they liked to fight! Our instructors were demanding about everything from academics to personal hygiene. I learned American history and I learned how to neatly fold my clothing so it could be stacked. That might not be a skill that has had much application in my life, but it was part of teaching my fellow cadets and me discipline, focus, and self-reliance.

The main rule was pretty simple: Do it right or do it again. One of my roommates from school told a reporter recently, "The school taught you how to be a leader. It taught you, 'show me a sore loser, and I'll show you a loser.' . . . Honesty and straightforwardness were the rule of law. It got ingrained in us that you don't lie, cheat, or steal, or tolerate those who do."

This may be why I never became a politician (until now)!

Our national educational system was never intended to be

limited to the three R's, history, and science. It was designed
to produce well-rounded young people capable of prospering
in the world. In addition to an education, kids were supposed
to graduate with some basic values, self-discipline, and life
skills. A little common sense wouldn't hurt either. Our schools
don't teach that anymore. Instead we're more concerned about
kids having self-esteem and feeling good about themselves
than we are about preparing them for real life. The politically
correct crowd has taken over our schools, and as a result we
are failing our children. And our children will fail America if
we don't do something about it. Educators are worried that
kids will feel bad if they flunk a test. You know what makes a
kid feel good?

Winning.

Succeeding.

We've dumbed down the curriculum to the lowest common denominator; in many schools, we've eliminated grading
entirely and diplomas have been practically devalued into cer-
tificates of attendance.

Our schools, our teachers, and our kids are capable of
more. A lot more.

The problem is we're taking the easy way out. Instead of
creating high standards and demanding more, we're expecting
less. We have to get tougher. Forget that self-esteem stuff; we
need to start challenging kids. We need to allow them to fail
when they don't work hard.

Anyone who has succeeded in business has survived a lot
of failure—but they were tough enough to get back up and try

again and again. Kids need to learn that success requires persistence. Self-esteem should come from overcoming challenges and surviving the hard knocks of trying to be better.

Yet today, some teachers and school administrators are more concerned about hurting their students' feelings or about hearing complaints from parents that they're being too tough. Instead of becoming more competitive, we're actually eliminating competition. That's incredible—and wrong.

Competition makes you stronger, it forces you to work harder, to do more. Corporations that can't compete with other companies go out of business, no matter how nice they are or how good they feel about themselves. Small businesses have the same challenge. The owners have to work hard and compete for their survival or they won't make it.

Competition is why I'm very much in favor of school choice. Let schools compete for kids. I guarantee that if you forced schools to get better or close because parents didn't want to enroll their kids there, they would get better. Those schools that weren't good enough to attract students would close, and that's a good thing.

For two decades I've been urging politicians to open the schoolhouse doors and let parents decide which schools are best for their children. Professional educators look to options such as school choice, charter schools, voucher programs, magnet schools, and opportunity scholarships.

Call them what you want—they all come down to the same thing: fostering competition.

Those people who are against offering parents choices

claim that doing so would be the end of good public schools. Better charter or magnet schools would drain the top kids out of that system, or hurt the morale of those left behind.

Suddenly, the excellence that comes from competition is being criticized.

Let's look at the facts. While the number of charter schools has grown substantially, they are still a small percentage of our public schools. But it looks like they are making a difference, especially in urban areas. Stanford University's Center for Research on Education Outcomes looked at the impact charter schools have made in 41 urban areas. They report that charter school students, compared to students in public schools, learn 40 days more advanced in math, and 28 more days in reading. That is significant, no matter how you look at it.

Look, I know that people both for and against school choice can roll out endless arguments and statistics showing charter schools are either very successful or make no difference at all. This is a legitimate debate. But anyone except a politician running for office and looking for support from the teacher unions has to realize that smaller class sizes, more individualized instruction, and stricter discipline all make a huge positive difference. Making teachers accountable is important, but we should stop measuring their performance with mindless standardized tests. We should be embracing the success stories and using them as a model for improving the others.

I'm not as concerned about the kids growing up in wealthy communities, where high property taxes have allowed them to build great schools, hire the best teachers, and provide all the supplies they need. Those schools are doing fine.

In many urban areas, however, schools must fight for every tax dollar and are forced to have teachers and students bring in their own basic supplies such as pencils and paper. That's a national tragedy.

The problem with public schools is that in many places there is no way to take an honest measurement of how they're doing. If a charter school isn't doing the job, it closes. That's the type of accountability we need throughout our educational system.

One huge obstacle is the strength of the teacher unions. Teacher unions don't want school choice because it means a potential reduction in union-protected jobs. In New York, for example, the unions have been so powerful for so long that, more than four decades ago, Woody Allen had a scene in his movie *Sleeper* in which a man wakes up in the future and is told that the world he'd known had been destroyed when the president of the powerful teachers union "got hold of a nuclear warhead." Thanks to strong contracts negotiated by the New York City teacher union, it's become almost impossible to discipline a teacher, much less actually fire one.

When there is a legitimate complaint against a teacher in the New York system, rather than having a quick hearing to determine the validity of the complaint, teachers are assigned to an area known as "the rubber room" while they wait for their hearing.

And they wait. They sit in empty classrooms or converted closets and do nothing—but they still get paid their whole salary. Some teachers spend several years waiting. No wonder they call it the rubber room—the whole concept is insane. But it's the result of the contracts that strong unions have forced on New York and other cities. When teacher unions fight against school choice the unions are saying that their product isn't good enough to compete in a free marketplace. Maybe they are right. And what about the good teachers? They can get stuck too and are at the mercy of the union.

These unions have a nice monopoly going, so why wouldn't they want to protect their turf? By the way, the teachers are not the only ones with troublesome unions. In New York City, the janitors don't arrive in the morning until exactly the same time as the students. That means the boiler might not be fired up yet, or doors might not be unlocked, so students have to wait outside.

To be upfront, I'm not a fan of the teacher unions, but I have great admiration and respect for teachers. Most of us can name a teacher or two who had a profound influence on our lives. But we've made teaching a tough profession. Good teachers love to teach. They respect and honor their profession. In too many classrooms, though, we've taken away their right to discipline disruptive kids, turning the teachers into babysitters as much as educators.

And a lot of good teachers aren't paid enough. It's an interesting choice we've made as a society. We entrust our kids to teachers for most of the daytime, where they'll have a really big impact on how their students will grow up. But we don't pay enough to attract the best people to the profession.

Unfortunately, teachers are not paid on merit. The standard for advancement is mostly the number of years of service— seniority. The really good and inspirational teachers burn out under the painful conditions found in too many schools. The bad teachers tend to hang around since they have nowhere else to go. Thus, the paychecks tend to be bigger for the less capable.

That's exactly the opposite of what we should be doing.

One way of making the profession more attractive is to put some discipline back in the school. A lot of our schools aren't safe. Putting metal detectors at the door may prevent kids from bringing in weapons, but it still doesn't prevent them from causing problems. We need to get a lot tougher on troublemakers. We need to stop feeling sorry for them. They are robbing other kids of time to learn.

I'm not saying we should go back to the days when teachers would get physical with students, but we need to restore rules about behavior in the classroom and hire trained security officers who can help enforce those rules. The parents or guardians must be brought into the process as well.

Most disciplinary problems among students begin in the home. All parents should ask themselves: What kind of example am I setting?

At the same time, there is nothing more important to the future of this country than our colleges and universities. We have the best higher-education system in the world. There is a reason that young people from all over the world come here to study at our schools.

The problem is that the cost of higher education is skyrocketing, making it so far out of reach that many potential students either can't afford it or have to take out huge loans to pay the tuition. Instead of making it easier for more of our young people to get the education they need, we're making it harder to access, and thus available to only the wealthier families.

My father succeeded without a college degree, but that would be much harder to do today. According to the Census Bureau, people with a bachelor's degree earn an average of $51,000 a year. That's $23,000 more a year than people with just high school diplomas and almost three times as much as high school dropouts.

When I speak at a college, the students surround me and ask me two questions: First, can I give or get them a job? And second, what can we do about their loans? They haven't even graduated from school, they haven't yet started working, and already they've mortgaged their future.

A four-year degree today can be expensive enough to create six-figure debt.

Getting an advanced degree or a medical education can put a young professional well over $100,000 to $200,000 in debt.

If the students can't get enough scholarships or loan support, the parents have to step in, despite the risks to their own retirement funds. They may have to borrow the money, often by taking out a second mortgage if they have sufficient value in their home.

We can't forgive these loans, but we should take steps to help them.

The big problem is the federal government. There is no reason the federal government should profit from student loans. This only makes an already difficult problem worse. The Federal Student Loan Program turned a $41.3 billion profit in 2013.

These student loans are probably one of the only things that the government shouldn't make money from and yet it does.

And do you think this has anything to do with why schools continue to raise their tuition every year? Those loans should be viewed as an investment in America's future.

In the end, we have no choice. We have to change the way we educate our children. We should return the basic control and responsibility for our schools to the states and local communities. They need to set standards for their teachers and students that reward competitive quality and excellence. Our communities have to make education a priority, with flexibility in the property taxes and other funding involved. And most important, the parents have to instill a spirit of discipline, focus, and passion for learning in their children because the schools can't do it alone.

We are living in a very competitive world. If we study how the Asian countries have taken over in so many of the technology-based industries, the handwriting is on the wall.

The future of our country is studying in our classrooms right now.

Making our education system work is an important step toward making America great again.

6

* * *

THE ENERGY DEBATE:
A LOT OF HOT AIR

AS OFTEN ATTRIBUTED TO Mark Twain, "Everybody talks about the weather, but nobody does anything about it." Apparently we're trying to prove him wrong.

We are actually blaming weather patterns on man-made causes. First, the so-called "experts" told us we were responsible for global warming, but then, when temperatures started dropping, scientists began referring to these variations as "climate change."

Now these "experts" can't figure out whether it's getting too hot or too cold, so the new term is "extreme weather conditions." That covers everything from boiling heat to frigid ice. However, the point is the same: By sending the by-products of burning fossil fuels into the atmosphere, we have supposedly changed the natural weather patterns.

In his 2015 State of the Union speech, President Obama declared the biggest threat on the planet today is climate change. The biggest threat?! We have ISIS troops chopping off the heads of innocent Christian missionaries. We have a coalition of adversaries in Syria supporting a dictator who uses chemical weapons on his own people. We have millions of Americans who have mortgages greater than the value of their property, while middle-class incomes are stagnant and more than 40 million citizens are living at poverty levels.

And our president is most concerned about climate change?

If you go back in history, you'll find that the biggest tornadoes we've had in this country took place in the 1890s, and the most hurricanes occurred in the 1860s and '70s. Violent climate "changes" are nothing new.

We have even had ice ages.

I just don't happen to believe they are man-made.

I do agree that so-called global climate change is causing us some problems: It's causing us to waste billions of dollars to develop technologies we don't need to fulfill our energy needs.

President Obama introduced a program known as "cap and trade," which sets a ceiling, or cap, on annual carbon dioxide emissions for companies. This would have forced them to reduce those emissions or pay a tax for the excess released above their cap. Because he could not get this legislation through the Congress, he has had his minions at the Environmental Protection Agency try to impose this plan through rule-making.

This plan has succeeded mostly in doing one thing—keeping oil at an inflated price. Even after oil has dropped to $50 a barrel, we still live with prices at the pump that are too high.

The truth is, we have sufficient energy supplies in this country to power us into the next century—all we have to do is develop them. Among all the gifts that God gave to America was an abundant supply of natural energy. According to the Department of Energy, the natural gas reserves we have in the ground could supply our energy needs for centuries.

For example, the Marcellus Shale Fields lying under New York, Pennsylvania, Ohio, and West Virginia could produce the equivalent of tens of billions of barrels of oil, giving us plenty of time to develop sensible and cheaper alternative forms of energy.

Right now, we are greatly dependent on oil. The cost of energy is one of the driving forces of our economy. Job creation is tied directly to the cost of oil. The more it costs to get it out of the ground and to the consumer, the fewer jobs that are created in all the industries that run on oil. We don't even know how much oil is sitting buried under your feet as you read this book right now.

Researchers at Rice University in Houston, Texas, have estimated we might have two trillion barrels of recoverable oil, enough to last the next 285 years. Technology has changed so much in the last few years that a Goldman Sachs study has estimated that by 2017 or 2018, we could overtake both Saudi Arabia and Russia to become the world's largest oil producer.

The oil is there for the taking; we just have to take it.

I've never understood why, with all of our own reserves, we've allowed this country to be held hostage by OPEC, the cartel of oil-producing countries, some of which are hostile to America. For the last few decades, the leaders of OPEC have been sitting around their conference table, setting the price of oil and laughing at us.

They know we have no leadership and we'll pay whatever price they conspire to create. For years I've been urging our politicians to have the guts to bust the OPEC cartel, but then I remember something else Twain said: "Suppose you were an idiot. And suppose you were a member of Congress. But I repeat myself."

We can't be fooled or lulled into a sense of security by the current drop in oil prices, which is unpredictable and still insufficient, given the amount of oil out there. Those oil prices are like the weather: guaranteed to change. We need to be prepared to drill our own oil. And we need to take advantage of every opportunity, including approving the Keystone XL Pipeline.

It's an outrage that Obama has delayed and probably even killed the 1,179-mile-long pipeline that would carry oil from Canada's tar sands to Nebraska, where it would connect to existing pipelines that would take it all the way to Texas, and at the same time create thousands of construction jobs. The excess of oil on the market, which has caused a great drop in prices, has made it seem less vital today, but eventually the world will need that oil, and we will need the good jobs that it will create.

One of the main criticisms of the pipeline has been the possibility of oil spills. Even the State Department has said the pipeline will be safe, and far better and safer than the existing system of transport. But mere possibilities shouldn't prevent progress. You prepare for these situations, taking as many precautions as possible, and when they occur, you clean them up.

We need to expand our own sources of oil, because the Middle East, our largest external source, is becoming more and more unstable. We still need Saudi Arabian oil, although we're less dependent on their product than we were only a few years ago.

But Saudi Arabia is a main target of or in some cases the home of terrorists. Given the Saudi overreliance on oil exports and their lack of a sustainable economy outside of oil, they are probably going to need our help at some point to stay in business. That's a real threat, which is why we need to reduce our foreign oil dependence considerably.

Our first priorities need to be approving the Keystone XL Pipeline and starting to drill everywhere oil is accessible.

There has been a big push to develop alternative forms of energy—so-called green energy—from renewable sources. That's another big mistake. To begin with, the whole push for renewable energy is being driven by the wrong motivation, the mistaken belief that global climate change is being caused by carbon emissions. If you don't buy that—and I don't—then what we have is really just an expensive way of making the tree-huggers feel good about themselves.

The most popular source of green energy is solar panels. They work, but they don't make economic sense. They don't provide enough energy savings to cover the cost of installing and using them. They are the most highly subsidized form of green energy in America.

Some estimates claim it takes as long as several decades after installing solar panels to get your money back. That's not exactly what I would call a sound investment.

Even if that number is only half right, what kind of investment do you make that takes 20 years before you break even? I understand solar energy is eventually going to become more efficient and maybe even cost-effective. Maybe. When it proves to be affordable and reliable in providing a substantial percent of our energy needs, then maybe it'll be worth discussing. Meanwhile, we have to keep our cars and trucks running and our homes and buildings heated. There are much more efficient, cost-effective, and reliable ways of doing that.

It's no secret that I've had serious personal issues with the supporters of wind turbines. For several years I battled the Scottish government over its plan to construct a really ugly wind farm consisting of eleven giant turbines right offshore of one of the most beautiful golf resorts in the world in Aberdeen.

The Trump International Golf Links Scotland resort in Aberdeen is a great tourist attraction that will benefit the Scottish economy and create jobs, while these turbines destroy some of the great beauty of the world.

There isn't sufficient wind power anyplace else?

To me, this policy never made sense. Even at its peak output the Scottish government was going to have to spend millions of pounds a year subsidizing this wind farm. We held up the project in court for almost five years and during that time the price of oil fell so drastically that this project no longer makes economic sense. So it is never going to be built. I did Scotland a big favor.

Like other countries, Scotland is trying to completely fulfill its energy needs from renewable sources within the next decade, but there is considerable skepticism about that plan. Bill Gates said flatly in 2015, "Renewable energy can't do the job. Governments should switch green subsidies into R&D." The cost to generate that much power from solar and wind energy would be, he said, "beyond astronomical." He told the *Financial Times* that the answer to supplying our future energy needs is going to come from technological breakthroughs yet to be achieved. Gates said he intended to invest as much as $2 billion in renewable energy research—but not in the development of wind and solar energy.

There are also a lot of questions about the damage that solar and wind power do to the environment. A recent study reported by a British think tank concluded that wind energy is "inordinately expensive and ineffective at cutting CO_2 emissions." Not only that, it added, "wind power, backed by conventional gas-fired generation, can emit more CO_2 than the most efficient gas turbines running alone"—and building these steel monsters, mostly in China, causes many pollutents.

Ironically, at the same time the wind farm in Scotland was going ahead, a similar project was denied approval in Doonbeg, Ireland, where I am building another beautiful resort. The plan there was to spoil the lavish views with nine 413-foot turbines—that's like lining up nine vertical football fields, including both end zones.

Fortunately, this plan was denied because the turbines might harm the estimated 7,000 freshwater pearl mussels, an endangered species on the European Union list, that were living in the Doonbeg River, and also be bad for tourism.

This magnificent golf course resort, absolutely one of the best in the world, was offering huge benefits to the local economy.

We were saved by mussels.

The bottom line is that we are going to remain dependent on

oil and natural gas to fill our energy needs for a long time into the future. So if we are going to become energy independent, we need to keep drilling. The good news is that we have tremendous supplies of fossil fuels. We just need to decide to go after it.

We need to use every cost-effective method we have available to retrieve these resources. That includes fracking. For those who don't know, fracking is a technology that involves injecting fluids into shale beds at a very high pressure to free locked-in resources. It makes it possible to recover vast amounts of oil and gas that otherwise can't be reached through traditional methods.

While New York governor Andrew Cuomo has banned fracking, this technology has created an economic boom in North Dakota, Pennsylvania, and Ohio. There were more jobs created and less unemployment in those areas than practically anywhere else in the country. Upstate New Yorkers would like to replicate that boom in their region, lower taxes, and pay off massive New York State debt.

The bottom line on energy is that until there is a better "alternate" or "green" way of supplying our energy needs, we must put our resources to work for us, and now.

7

★ ★ ★

HEALTH CARE IS
MAKING US ALL SICK

THE BASIC DIFFERENCE BETWEEN the politicians' way and my way is that I've actually had to *do* the things that politicians only *talk about doing.*

I've hired thousands of employees. I've had to negotiate with contractors and unions. I've had to provide health care coverage for my workers. I know what the real costs are, I know what the problems are. I know what works and what doesn't work.

Most important, I know where the waste is and how to provide good medical coverage at reasonable costs.

Politicians don't want to hear the truth, nor do they want to tell you the truth. They're total hypocrites, especially when campaigning for reelection. They love to take to the stump and condemn "reckless government spending" and "government waste." And yet virtually every bill passed by Congress is loaded with special goodies for their districts.

We call this the "pork barrel" approach, which is a real disservice to pigs, who are only eating to survive. The pork barrel in politics is creating government waste in order to reward some special donor or interest group or to mollify a cranky member of Congress in return for his or her vote.

And we're paying for it.

I get very angry when I think about how our "Affordable Care" Act was rammed down a lot of sore throats by the Democrats.

Even Nancy Pelosi, the Democratic House Majority Leader at the time, conceded that most supporters of the bill had not actually read it.

Clearly, the public didn't understand what "Obamacare" was providing: its complexity, its concessions to the insurance lobby, its taking away of the right to keep your current physicians, and, naturally, the hidden, escalating costs of health care, especially for state treasuries and businesses of all sizes. And for individuals who are young and healthy, there's no way out of it without paying a fine.

Virtually all Republicans—and a growing number of Democrats—realize this is already a disaster that will only get worse. Premiums are skyrocketing—up 30 percent to 50 percent—and that will only get worse.

Look, I'm lucky. I'm able to afford the best health care in the world for myself and my family and my employees. I know that, but I also know that most people can't do that and need some help. This is a subject that has been really important to me for a very long time.

There's no question. Obamacare is a catastrophe, and it has to be repealed and replaced. And it was only approved because President Obama lied 28 times saying you could keep your doctor and your plan—a fraud and the Republicans should have sued—and meant it. As the different provisions kick in over the next few years, individual deductibles are going to continue to rise. People will have to get hit by a truck to be eligible for coverage because those deductibles are going to be so high.

Medical people hate it.

Doctors are quitting all over the place.

I have a friend who is one of the best doctors in the country. You would know the names of many of his patients. He told me, "Donald, I've never seen anything like this. I can't practice medicine the way I want to anymore. I have more accountants and computer programmers working for me than I have nurses." He's right. There are now more than 100 codes for doctors to get reimbursement from insurance companies.

We've turned the "paperwork" or "computer folders" in our medical system into the same nightmare as our 80,000-page tax code.

As I've repeatedly said, the "un-Affordable" Care Act has to be replaced. Where I differ from what others say—as usual—is in the way I would change it. Many years ago, long before anybody else was talking about it, I knew we had to make changes in the system. I knew it because I saw what effect health care costs were having on the bottom line. I knew it because at that time we had more than 40 million Americans without any insurance at all, and now we are forcing "part-time" jobs down the system.

I said then that we needed to find a plan for everyone that was affordable, well-administered, and that provided freedom of choice. You know, a plan that actually allows you to keep your doctor if you want to. At that time I talked about a single-payer plan which, in our then much less complicated system, may have had a chance of working. But it was only one of several suggestions from a nonpolitician at a time when many different concepts and ideas also were discussed. This was 15 years ago, but it still gets brought up a lot by other people. I guess they have nothing new to complain about. As usual, because they have no solutions of their own, they resort to "gotcha politics," which gets us nowhere closer to solving this problem or any other. They are all talk and no action. The Affordable Care Act is a clear example of that.

To succeed in business, you have to be flexible and you have to change with the realities of the world. The world has changed; I've changed. I don't think a single-payer system makes sense anymore. If I did, I would say it; I wouldn't need anyone else to say it for me. Maybe a single-payer system works in other countries. It works incredibly well in Scotland, for example, and maybe it could have worked here at a different time.

But not anymore.

So what can we do about it? There's no question we need real health care reform. We can't let Americans go without health care because they don't have the right resources. Sadly, that statement might cost me—but I still believe Republicans have big, beautiful "hearts" and want to help the poor and the sick—and can do so at the right price. I can't even imagine what it must be like to be sick and unable to go to a doctor. This only throws people back into emergency rooms that are overcrowded and inefficient already.

The Census Bureau has reported that 10 million people have now been added to the system. We have to find a way to take care of those people who can't take care of themselves. I believe that very strongly—even if it costs me.

I know Americans agree with me, because wherever I go in Ohio, Florida, Iowa, South Carolina, and New Hampshire, when I say it, people give me a standing ovation. The real argument is how do we take care of those who cannot take care of themselves? How do we make sure Americans have access to good health care so that our kids get everything they need, and that even people who can't afford the basic programs get at least reasonable care?

To me, for politicians to claim that we have an answer to every problem is silly. When you listen to some politicians reeling off their prepared answers, you almost fall for it. They're so smart that they already have a solution to every problem, and it's always better than everyone else's solutions. How convenient. But not for our country, because nothing gets done. Nothing gets solved, and we don't win. What I hear is a lot of ridiculous promises from politicians about how they intend to fix everything. They're all experts. But nothing ever happens. They're all talk and no action.

Most of them have gotten really good at saying absolutely

nothing. They've all got some kind of program, but when you listen to them, you still don't know what they're talking about.

My approach is completely different. I approach complicated problems such as how to provide health care for most Americans at a price we can afford the same way I solve the toughest business problems. We should hire the most knowledgeable people in the world on this subject and lock them in a room—and not unlock the door until they've agreed on the steps we need to take.

A lot of times when I speak, people say I don't provide specific policies that some pollster has determined are what people want to hear. I know that's not the way the professional politicians do it—they seem to poll and focus-group every word. But there's nobody like me.

Nobody.

I ask people to look at what I've done throughout my whole career. Look at how successful I've been doing things my way. So they have a choice: They can pretend some impossible solution is actually going to happen, or they can listen to the person who has proved that he can solve problems.

I started in a relatively small real estate company based in Brooklyn and made more than $10 billion. I now live on what is considered the best block of real estate anywhere in the world—Fifth Avenue between 56th Street and 57th Street, right next to Tiffany's in the heart of New York City.

That doesn't mean I don't have some ideas about the right approach to take. First of all, we cannot cut either Social Security or Medicare benefits. That's off the table. Those programs can be saved by growing the economy. Second, there are some simple changes that would provide real benefits.

As I've said, I'd like to see a private insurance system without artificial lines drawn between states. We need to get rid of those lines and let people and companies cross state lines to purchase the best plan for them. The government should get out of the way and let insurance companies compete for your business.

I have a big company. I have thousands of employees. If I'm negotiating for health insurance for my people in New York or California or Texas, I usually have one bidder in each state. Competition brings down prices, and the way the law is now, it discourages real competition between insurance companies for customers. They have virtual monopolies within the states. That makes no sense. It's very stupid and unfair for us.

You know who loves a lack of competition? Those insurance companies, who are making a fortune because they control the politicians. They've paid for them with their contributions, and it's a good investment from their perspectives. For our country, not so much. They give money to almost all the politicians. I'm using my own money so I am free to do what's right, and serve the people, not the lobbyists.

Nobody understands business better than I do. You want better plans at a better price? Increase competition for customers.

The government doesn't belong in health care except as the very last resort. The main way the government should be involved is to make sure the insurance companies are financially strong so that if there is a catastrophic event or they make some kind of miscalculation, they have the resources they'll need to handle it.

If we follow my logic, our health care system, and our economy, will be well again very soon.

8

★　　★　　★

IT'S STILL THE ECONOMY, STUPID

ALL THE PUNDITS, AND just about everyone else, said I would never really run for the presidency. When I announced I was a candidate for president, some of those same people predicted it wasn't really going to happen. They were sure I would drop out of the race before submitting my financial disclosures.

Apparently they thought I would be embarrassed to admit that I was not as wealthy as most people thought. But after filing those papers they found out I was worth much more.

I'm rich. I mean, I'm *really* rich. I've earned more money than even I thought I would—and I've had some pretty big dreams.

You know, I hear politicians talk, and they say things like "I was a constitutional law professor, so I'm an expert on the

Constitution." Or maybe they say, "I was on the Senate Foreign Relations committee for 25 years, so that makes me an expert on foreign policy." They point out how "successful" they were when they were CEO of a great company—where they cut 30,000 jobs, many of which ended up overseas, thus making them experts on job creation—experts on sending jobs *outside* of America to replace jobs *inside* of America.

I listen to these people talking about how they are going to fix our economy, how they are going to create jobs, how they are going to lower taxes and balance the budget. I shake my head and I think, You wouldn't have even qualified to be a contestant on *The Apprentice.*

We shouldn't take any fiscal advice from members of a Congress that can't pass a budget, nor should we expect them to keep their job-creating promises. We need someone who is a tough negotiator and a real leader. Sadly, the Republican majority doesn't possess the leadership or the negotiating skills necessary to pass a budget that would eliminate programs that ought to be entirely in private hands, or even eliminated completely.

The only time they really stand up to Obama, and then they fold, is in the final days when spending authorizations are running out. Where were they this summer when the real work and consensus could have been developed?

They're going to screw up the lives of millions of Americans—and destroy our credit rating—because they don't have the leadership skills needed to make our country great again and to look out for Americans.

What we are confronted with is a mixture of bad management and bad politics.

We need leadership in the White House that will keep government functioning while getting the feds out of all the areas where they don't belong. If the government is properly sized and properly focused, we won't need to go from crisis to crisis.

We need to start with the United States Congress. We've had presidents (Lyndon Johnson for one; Ronald Reagan for another) who have managed to build consensus and get things done. When President Reagan fired the air traffic controllers during his seventh month in office, he sent a signal to the unions that they heard loud and clear. When President Johnson twisted arms to get enough votes for the passage of a civil rights bill, he took on the far left and the far right and threatened them in order to get his way.

It can be done.

President Obama is big on playing golf. But he doesn't play with the right people. He should be playing with those smart people who can help our country, establishing bonds to get things done—and not just his friends.

Believe me, I know how to use a golf course—and golf clubs—to make deals. The only things that work are having a clear point of view and knowing how to get your message across to the country so that the people support and understand your mission. This way we're not divided, and special interest groups cannot buy the outcomes they want and rip us apart.

It all comes down to leadership. I don't think many people would disagree that I tell it like it is. When you see the coverage of me on television, in newspapers, and on social media, you'd have to agree that I get more attention for my opinions than all the other Republican candidates put together. Hopefully, that's respect and not pure entertainment—but it may be a little of both.

I manage to blast through the ridiculous liberal bias of the media and speak right to the hearts of the people—or at least I try. Even *New York* magazine, hardly a conservative outlet, has given me credit on its cover for shaking up the status quo.

Again, we're talking leadership.

When it comes to creating jobs and straightening out our economy, I am the only expert who isn't talking in "theory." I talk common sense and practical realism learned from the school of hard knocks. I've been there, done that, suffered through adversity, gone into debt, fought back, and come out on top, and much biggger and stronger than ever before. During the Recession of 1990 many of my friends went bankrupt, and never recovered. I never went bankrupt. I survived, and learned so much about how to deal with bad times. Our country is going through a bad time—I get it, and I know how to solve it.

I'm a fighter. Knock me down, and I come back even stronger. I love it!

I've spent my entire life not just making money but, more importantly, learning how to manage my resources and share them with the thousands who have worked for me. To hear our left-wing critics tell it, we need socialism to make this country move forward, and we need a president who can make up the rules as he goes along. If he can't get Congress to do something, he needs to rule by executive order.

I say that's complete nonsense.

The free market works—it just needs leadership, not dictatorship. Our government needs to employ a strong adherence to the Constitution and maintain social programs that inspire and reward achievement and that are constantly accountable for their spending and outcomes. I'm very concerned about the 46.5 million people living in poverty, and the great majority of middle-class Americans who can barely afford their homes (or have lost them). I am very concerned for the people who can't pay for the education of their children. In short, I am concerned for the people who can't buy into the American dream because the financial programs of this country are so tilted in favor of the rich.

That's why one of my strongest ideas is to look at the tax code in both its complexity and its obvious bias toward the rich. Hedge fund and money managers are important for our pension funds and the 401(k) plans that help millions of Americans—but far less important than they think. But financial advisers should pay taxes at the highest levels when they're earning money at those levels. Often, these financial engineers are "flipping" companies, laying people off, and making billions—yes, billions—of dollars by "downsizing" and destroying people's lives and sometimes entire companies. Believe me, I know the value of a billion dollars—but I also know the importance of a single dollar.

The money I've earned was the result of my own work— projects I created, deals I made, companies I bought and turned around. I understand what it means for my employees to work in construction, one of the toughest and most dangerous jobs in the world.

Those who spend their days sweating at their job should not have to sweat about their lives at night.

I've never had the "security" of being on the government payroll. I was the guy who made out the payroll. It hasn't always been so easy either. In the 1990s, the government changed the real estate tax laws and made those changes retroactive. It was very unfair, but I fought through it and thrived. It absolutely killed the construction industry. It put a lot of people out of business. The misguided passion of environmentalists today makes building anything much more difficult. Now we have crazy overregulation. You can barely buy a paper clip without being in violation of some governmental policy.

It's no surprise that stress in our society is at an all-time high. Let good and fair-minded businessmen and business-women run their companies, especially small businesses, without so much interference. Then they can make more money, put more people to work—and not just part-timers forced in by Obamacare—and have happier lives for themselves.

Right now this country is in serious financial trouble. Our national debt is more than $19 trillion, and we're on our way to $20 trillion. Even the most liberal economists warn that as we head past the $20+ trillion debt levels, we'll be in big, big trouble. That's when our financial system really starts to falter and diminish our borrowing capacity as well as drive up the interest costs on our debt.

That's when we will lose a lot of credibility in the world markets. For the past year, the United States has been the one country that has maintained financial stability while Europe and Asia faltered. Our debt is a very dangerous burden to carry around. There are overwhelming numbers of Americans who have not participated in the economic growth of the past year, or of the past 20 years, for that matter. They are being forced to mortgage their dreams—their American dreams—just to maintain where they are—just to get by. They have little or no hope of getting ahead.

This is a case where our system is broken, and we need to fix it. We've got to do something to change the way we're developing policy, and we've got to start right now. We need people who understand the scope of the problems and know how to turn the ship of state around.

We need leadership!

Some of the proposed solutions make no sense. There are politicians who think one way of reducing the national debt is to cut Social Security or other entitlement programs. We have to tread very carefully here. Since our "great" depression more than 80 years ago, America has always provided a social safety net for those who fall off the economic chart. Retired seniors in particular rely on pensions and Social Security, as well as Medicare.

We have to be very careful about changing the rules for those whose monthly checks make a big difference in their survival. A lot of people live from check to check. There's no way I'm letting those payments be reduced. No way. This country made a deal with our citizens. That's their money. They paid it into the system their whole working lives so that older people could get their monthly checks.

Now it's their turn.

We should not touch Social Security. It's off the table.

But you know what? There are a lot of wealthy people who don't need it. So if the government offered me the opportunity to give it up, I would check that box. I'm sure there are other wealthy individuals who would do the same thing. Even so, the impact that would have on solving the financial crisis we face would be minimal.

Changing the tax code to be more fair for all income classes is a much better answer to this bigger problem.

There are certainly "entitlements" that can be reviewed for waste and misguided direction or wasteful execution. I discuss immigration policies elsewhere, but I question whether illegal immigrants—or their children—should be receiving the same benefits as bona fide citizens or those who are here lawfully.

At the same time, government largesse for many businesses and industries—"entitlements for the rich"—needs to be examined. I am very suspicious of income-supplement programs that seem to expand for industries with large lobbying teams or for companies run by major contributors to election campaigns.

To solve our overall economic problem, we have to start rebuilding our industries to meet the challenge from foreign competitors and create real jobs. Government statistics are made to look very positive, but in real life the situation is terrible.

When you look at the unemployment situation, there are two very significant variables. One is the percentage of people who give up and drop out of the labor market. They aren't in-

cluded in the unemployment sample. Our so-called labor par-
ticipation rate—those who have stayed in the job market—is
the lowest it's been in almost 40 years. It hasn't been this low
since President Jimmy Carter was running the country, and
he presided over an inflationary spiral in which interest rates
exceeded 20 percent.

When you also take into account the large number of job-
holders who are underemployed, the real unemployment rate
soars to the high teens or even 20 percent. I know many wise
financial heads question the government's assessment of the
job market and the statistics it puts out. In our daily lives, we
see from our friends and neighbors that the job market is still
very troubled, as downsizing continues to be a popular buzz-
word for corporations trying to hype their stock.

It's not just jobs that are being lost to other countries. We
are seeing whole industries vanish overseas.

Americans want to work. We have a great work ethic in this
country. The problem is that when young people look for their
first good jobs, or people who have lost their jobs look for new
ones, they can't find any.

The jobs aren't there. They've vanished!

I've certainly done my part in my businesses. I know how
to create jobs. I have created tens of thousands of jobs in my
career. Thousands of people currently work for me and many
thousands more are employed by my partnerships. I'm involved
in literally hundreds of companies, almost all of which are
working beautifully, and setting new standards and records.

They include everything from a bottled springwater
company to a vineyard. We manage ice-skating rinks, we pro-

duce TV shows, we make leather goods, we create fragrances, and we own beautiful restaurants.

Of course, our bread-and-butter is in our bricks-and-mortar or real estate. We own, build, manage, and/or license many beautiful buildings of all types.

There is only one thing that every single one of my many different businesses have in common: They all help provide jobs for people. When I construct a building or develop a golf resort, it creates jobs for construction workers and for all the companies supplying the materials, from the flooring to the lighting fixtures.

These are good jobs.

When a building is finished and occupied, or when people are playing on one of my golf courses, or staying at a hotel, we supply the service personnel who keep these businesses running.

More good jobs.

The same thing is true with having my products made in China or Mexico or other countries. Some have attacked me for urging that we complain about these countries at the same time I'm having goods manufactured there.

My response: I'm a realist. I'm a competitor.

When I am working on a business deal, I make the best deal. But we should be changing the business climate so that manufacturers can get the best deal *right here in the US*. Right now it doesn't work that way.

We need legislation that gives American companies the tax priorities and financial support to create more of their technology and to redirect more of their manufacturing here at home.

We must stop certain countries from devaluing their currency at the drop of a hat.

We're the home team, and we should come first.

So how do we get back the jobs we've lost to other countries?

Answer: Start by negotiating better trade agreements with our "friendly" partners.

We have to bring jobs back from places like China, Japan, and Mexico. We have to stand up and be tough. In too many ways we're giving away the greatest market in the world—the American consumer.

Ford recently announced that it's building a $2.5 billion plant in Mexico. Nabisco is moving a big plant from Chicago to Mexico. A German auto company was all set to build a plant in Tennessee, but then it changed its mind and is building it in Mexico instead.

How does that happen? How many good jobs did we lose in just those two deals? How many more deals like that have slipped through our fingers without our even realizing it? Hundreds, maybe even thousands, but no more!

It's ridiculous. We all know that the American labor force is the best there is. We just have to allow them to compete.

But we sit there while we're getting beaten in trade agreements. In my companies, we fight for every deal. We fight for the best price on cleaning materials for the restaurants and the best price for the printing of the labels on our wine bottles.

I fight for my people every day.

Now I am fighting for America. I want our country to start winning again. And we can!

All it takes is a commitment to winning and making "Made in America" a badge of honor just like it used to be.

9

★　★　★

NICE GUYS CAN FINISH FIRST

I'M A NICE GUY. I really am. But I have a nasty habit that most career politicians don't have: I tell the truth. I'm not afraid to say exactly what I believe. When I'm asked a question, I don't answer with a speech that ignores a controversial subject. I answer the question.

Sometimes people don't like my answers. Too bad.

So they attack me. And when someone attacks me, I fight back. Hard.

That has always been my philosophy: If my critics attack me, then I'll fight back. Let's be honest and truthful with one another. I'm confident my answer makes the most sense.

You know who really appreciates this approach? The American people.

They're not used to hearing the truth from politicians, but they love it, and they love hearing it from me.

They have never seen anyone like me in politics. They have never seen anyone who is willing to stand up to the lobbyists, the PACs, the special interests, who all have way too much influence over Washington politicians. I am paying my own way so I can say whatever I want. I will only do what is right for our country, which I love.

Sometimes there is a price I pay for that. Loyalty is extremely important to me. My family and close friends will say that I am loyal to a fault. That's why, when I announced that I was running, I was very interested to see which of my so-called friends would remain loyal to me.

In politics, 55 percent of the vote is considered a landslide—but that means 45 percent of the people are against you. I've never had 45 percent against me. When I went to events, people would cheer, I would hear very few boos or hecklers. But when you run for political office, suddenly you hear some boos in the background. One night, at a charity event where I had made a major contribution, my wife, Melania, was with me as I was cheered loudly. But we were surprised to hear a small number of people booing in the background. Melania said to me, "Darling, do you know what? You've never been booed before." I looked at her and said, "Welcome to the world of politics."

In fact, I have been surprised by some people I once considered friends. One of my biggest surprises was Macy's. I've had a long and good relationship with the chairman and CEO, Terry Lundgren—a very nice guy and good executive. I've sold shirts, ties, cuff links, and fragrances at Macy's. We've done very well. I like the fact that Trump was the only brand that could sell a $50 million apartment and a $37 tie.

Terry Lundgren was a good friend. We spent a lot of time together at Mar-a-Lago and at many Trump golf courses. I've introduced him to people who have become good friends of his. I got a call from him in August 2015 when I was receiving a lot of bad press regarding my statements about illegal immigration. I was getting ready to speak to a large crowd in New Hampshire when my cell phone rang. The emcee on the dais had already started introducing me—he was talking about some of my buildings, how well I was doing in the polls. But when I saw Terry—a friend—was calling, I answered.

"Donald, Donald, I have to speak to you," he said in a rushed and nervous tone. "We're receiving calls from Mexicans. They're going to picket Macy's."

I said, "That's no big deal. They'll be there for an hour."

"I can't let this happen," he said. "It wouldn't be good for our company's reputation."

I told him I was getting ready to make a speech and couldn't talk to him, but said pointedly, "If you do this, it would truly be an act of disloyalty because you're getting a little bit of heat over selling my ties and shirts. Aside from that, it wouldn't make me look very good."

Terry said, "I've got to do something. We're putting out a press release that we're terminating you." Wow, I thought to myself, and this is a company that just paid a massive fine for some terrible acts to its customers. Not nice!

As he read the release the emcee announced my name and the crowd roared. "Wait a second. You're reading this while

I have to speak to this packed house? Can't it wait until to-morrow?"

"We have to do it now," he said. "It can't wait."

"Wow. What a great act of disloyalty. I'm telling you that if they picket, they'll be there for an hour. Nobody cares."

My ties, shirts, cuff links, and fragrances are now available at Trump Tower, not at Macy's. I've been told that many thou-sands of people cut up their Macy's credit cards and mailed them back to the store because of this. The public gets it.

I've also heard that other companies have stopped doing business with Macy's. And at least one prominent businessman told me, "I can't believe how disloyal Terry Lundgren was." He added jokingly, "He used Mar-a-Lago more than you do!"

Likewise, NBC and Univision refused to broadcast the Miss Universe/Miss USA Pageants. I sued NBC, but settled after buy-ing its half of the company and selling the whole thing to IMG. Currently I am suing Univision for a substantial amount of money.

I'd had a long and very successful relationship with NBC, which made millions broadcasting my top-rated show, *The Ap-prentice*. But before this happened I'd told them that if I ran for president, because of the equal-time regulations, I would not be doing the show anymore. *The Apprentice* had already been renewed and top executives of NBC and Comcast came to my office to try to convince me to change my mind.

Steve Burke of Comcast, NBC's president Bob Greenblatt, and Paul Telegdy, head of reality television, are great guys, and my relationship with all of them has been an amazing experi-ence. I'm so glad we settled our litigation, and life goes on.

My lawsuit against Univision continues though, and at

some point I expect to win a lot of money from them. They broke a contract and for that they must pay. It's sad because I had such a great liking for the two top executives, Randy Falco and Beau Ferrari. Who knows? At some point we'll probably have that relationship again.

The publicity about severing ties those first few weeks was relentless: ESPN BREAKS TIES WITH TRUMP—even though I never had a deal with ESPN. They were using my golf course on the Pacific Ocean, Trump National Los Angeles, for a golf outing. NASCAR CUTS ALL TIES WITH TRUMP—but I had no ties with NASCAR, they were renting a ballroom at Trump National Doral for their annual banquet. And, in fact, I kept their substantial deposits and will rent those places to someone else—hopefully for more money.

Things have calmed down and people are now giving me great credit for raising the problem of illegal immigration. I made that issue so important because it is so important to the future of America. I wasn't surprised it caused a lot of problems. Most politicians don't want to get too close to something that controversial. I don't care. I learned how to be direct, how to be honest, and how to stand up for my beliefs from my father.

Fred Trump, my wonderful, tough but loving father, built, owned, and managed buildings in Queens and Brooklyn. He made enough money to just sit back and relax, but that wasn't who he was. Even on weekends he'd be walking through a building, a house, or a construction site. If the halls were dirty or a bulb was out, the people working there would know about it. My father wasn't overly concerned with hurting someone's feelings—he wanted the floors to be cleaned or, as he would often say, in "mint condition." If the person responsible couldn't keep them clean, he was gone. My father believed he had an obligation to his tenants. His motto was simple: You do your job, you keep your job. Do it well, you get a better job. That always made sense to me.

Unfortunately, politics doesn't work that way. In politics, once someone gets elected, it's tough to get them out. There's no motivation to try to get anything done. If the American public had any idea what really goes on, they'd be much angrier than they are already. Congress's approval rating would be even lower than it is now. Career politicians like it this way; being a politician is their career. I know many of them; believe me, they couldn't get a job in private industry. They don't want anyone taking away their great pension plan and health benefits—that *you* are paying for.

The special interests and lobbyists also like it this way. They're earning a lot of money selling influence—and giving away money is a lot easier than cleaning floors. Believe me, I know how it works, I've made a lot of campaign contributions.

I'm not taking a penny from those people. I'm paying my own way. So the old rules don't apply to me—and those people who benefit from those rules don't know how to react. At first they hoped if they ignored me I would go away. The American people certainly proved them wrong. They love the fact that someone is finally standing up for their interests!

They couldn't ignore me, so they started attacking me. These veteran politicians looked for the place I was most vulnerable—which is why they attacked my hair, which is mine, by the way. They showed a lot of courage attacking my hair; this resulted in what might be the strangest political headline ever written when NBC News reported: TRUMP DEFENDS HAIR, ATTACKS MEDIA AT CAMPAIGN RALLY!

Recently though, they have been claiming I haven't put out enough specifics. There's a good reason for this, and it fits perfectly with my overall philosophy of leadership: Many of our problems, caused by years of stupid decisions or no decisions at all, have grown into a huge mess. If I could wave a magic wand and fix them, I'd do it. But there are a lot of different voices—and interests—that have to be considered when working toward solutions. This involves getting people into a room and negotiating compromises until everyone walks out of that room on the same page.

No one likes to compromise. Believe me, I will never compromise on the basic principles I'm discussing in this book. Yet every party to a decision needs to feel his position is understood. The hardest part of putting up a building is getting the city officials, the city council, the environmentalists, local zoning boards, and the ever-critical media to agree that this was an acceptable project. Then we have to bring in the banks, the contractors, and the unions to make sure the project is financially feasible.

If I'd said at the beginning, "This is exactly the way we're going to construct this building," the headlines would have announced: MAJOR OPPOSITION TO NEW TRUMP PROJECT! Nothing would get done.

The same principles apply to management of the federal government. Congress can't pass a budget because no one knows how to negotiate with the various interests involved in funding our government. Most of the time Congress simply accepts last year's spending, which was a continuation of the previous year's spending. That is followed by an agreement on an emergency temporary stopgap measure. There is no final resolution, so the same broken process is repeated year after year.

We need to find the best people, including experts in various fields and economists, as well as congressional leaders to provide perspective and determine which programs are working and should be kept or expanded, which programs should be cut, and what new programs might be added to deal with the changing world. Career politicians always claim to have these answers—but how is that possible when they haven't properly analyzed the situation?

A great leader has to be flexible, holding his ground on the major principles but finding room for compromises that can bring people together. A great leader has to be savvy at negotiations so we don't drown every bill in pork barrel bridges to nowhere. I know how to stand my ground—but I also know that Republicans and Democrats need to find common ground to stand on as well.

We need to see more real achievements in the first 100 days of the next administration than we've seen in the seven years of the Obama presidency. Washington needs to get moving in the right direction again. Hopefully you will understand that is more important than all the wonky details of grand plans that will never be enacted.

And by the way, I have outlined plenty of policy initiatives. This is not "the politics of hope." This is "the politics of reality," which only a strong businessman like me can develop.

Another favorite gimmick my opponents use to attack my ideas is to claim I'm not a conservative, or not even a Republican. Or worse, I'm not a politician! They claim this makes it impossible for me to get things done in Washington.

I've got news for them: *Washington doesn't work.*

Ironically, it was this type of criticism that helped my ideas attract attention and gain popularity in the first place. The contrast reminded Americans what they really think of career politicians.

As for being a Republican and conservative, let me tell you a story about how our political system really works. In May 2015 the president of a major conservative advocacy group, the Club for Growth, came up to my office in Trump Tower. He seemed like a very nice, reasonable guy. During that meeting he said some very complimentary things about my business success and told me that people like me were needed in Washington.

A week later we received a letter from him reading, "As we both know, it is business owners who create jobs—not the government." Then he asked for a million-dollar donation.

A million dollars!

When I turned him down he attacked me in the press. I was not a real candidate, he said, "and it would be unfortunate if I took away a spot at even one Republican debate."

Take away a spot from whom? Someone, I suspect, who gave them that big donation.

When I pulled ahead in the polls, this group spent a million dollars on ads attacking me in Iowa. This is one smart group; they come to my office asking for a million-dollar donation— and it ends up costing them a million dollars.

Meanwhile they're bad-mouthing me to their followers: "Donald Trump is the worst kind of politician who will say anything to get elected." Saying anything to them means telling the truth to me.

This demonstrates everything that is wrong with our political system. We look at politicians and think: This one's owned by this millionaire. That one's owned by that millionaire, or lobbyist, or special interest group.

Me? I speak for the people.

So the establishment attacks me. They can't own me, they can't dictate to me, so they search for ways to dismiss me. They point out (accurately, for once) that at one time I was a registered Democrat. I grew up and worked in New York, where virtually everyone is a Democrat.

You know who else was a Democrat? Ronald Reagan. He switched, and I switched years ago, when I began to see what liberal Democrats were doing to our country. Now I'm a conservative Republican with a big heart. I didn't decide to become a Republican. That's who I have always been.

By nature, I'm a conservative person. I believe in a strong work ethic, traditional values, being frugal in many ways and aggressive in military and foreign policy. I support a tight interpretation of the Constitution, which means judges should stick to precedent and not write social policy.

I represent traditional conservative values. I get up every morning and go to work. I work hard, I've been honest and I'm very successful. The billions I have? I earned every penny. When I was beginning my career my father never gave me much money, but he gave me a great work ethic. I always know a hater when they say my father gave me $200 million when I was starting out. I only wish!

Number one: He didn't have that kind of money. In those days, all of Brooklyn wasn't worth $200 million. And number two: If he did, he would never have given it to me.

When I wanted to leave Brooklyn and Queens and venture into Manhattan, he thought I was crazy. Nevertheless he had confidence in me. I'll never forget when he told my incredible mother, "Look, I don't know if he is right or wrong, but I've got to let him do it. He has great ability and talent, and who knows? He may be able to pull it off." My father was a tough cookie, but he had a warm heart. He was a man who truly loved his wife and five children: Maryanne, Elizabeth, Robert, Fred, and me. He always wanted what was best for us.

He loaned me a small amount of money—loaned, not gave—around $1 million—money that I probably could have gotten from a bank—and the biggest part of my journey began. I paid my father back a few years later, with full interest, after my Manhattan deals started to come in—and very successfully. One of them, the Grand Hyatt Hotel, was a big hit, built by me—on time and under budget. I made a lot of money. He was very happy and even more proud of me than ever before.

When my father passed away at the age of 93, he left his estate to his children. By that time, I had already built a massive and internationally recognized company. After the family split the assets and estate taxes, the money I got was—relative to what I had built—not that consequential. Nice to have but not a big-money factor. What he left me, much more importantly, were the best "genes" that anybody could get. He was a special man and father.

Let's review the conservative scorecard and check my grades:

Affordable health care? Here's my word—and I never go

back on my word: Obamacare needs to be repealed ASAP—and replaced with something far better.

Immigration reform? Has anybody been more of a leader on this issue than me? My plan is simple: We build a wall and take back control of our country. Massive law enforcement on the borders. Legal immigrants should speak or learn English; without it they can never assimilate.

Anchor babies? They're here for one day and the child is entitled to a lifetime of benefits when others have spent a lifetime, or their lives, earning them. This needs to end!

The Iran deal? Iran cannot be allowed to build a nuclear weapon. That's not a threat. It's a statement of fact. Our allies and foes alike should take heed.

The Second Amendment? I believe the rights of law-abiding gun owners must be fully protected.

Defense of religious freedom? I believe religious freedom is the most fundamental constitutional right we have and must be protected.

Fix our broken tax system? There is no politician who understands our tax system like I do. It has to be changed to make it fair for all Americans—and simplified.

I am a strong, proud conservative. The biggest difference between me and all the do-nothing politicians who are all talk, no action? Those people constantly claiming they are more conservative than anyone else? I don't talk about things, I get things done.

I am standing up for this country because our so-called leaders haven't been able to. So the next time someone questions my conservative credentials, show them this list!

10

★　★　★

LUCKY TO BE AN AMERICAN

I KNOW HOW LUCKY I am. The day I was born I had already won the greatest lottery on Earth. I was born in the United States of America. With that came the amazing opportunities that every American citizen has: The right to become the best possible person you can be. The right to be treated equally with all other Americans. The right to speak freely (and by the way I take that right *very* seriously). The right to practice the religion of your choice the way you choose. The right to achieve as much as your own hard work and talent allow. The right to be secure in your home thanks to the greatest law enforcement agencies anywhere, and the privilege of raising your family knowing that you are protected by the men and women of the finest military forces in the world.

I think my parents must have known how proud I would be to be an American: I was born on Flag Day, June 14!

I'll tell you how proud I am to be an American. You may have heard that I own a house in Palm Beach, Florida. It's called Mar-a-Lago, which means "Sea to Lake." It has 128 rooms. It's listed as a National Historic Landmark because it is one of the most beautiful homes ever built. It was built by E. F. Hutton and his cereal heiress wife, Marjorie Merriweather Post, in 1927.

The land it sits on is reportedly the most valuable 20 acres of land in Florida. After I bought it, I wanted people to know how proud and grateful I am to be an American, so I decided to fly an American flag in front of my house, an American flag that nobody could miss, a flag fitting for this beautiful house.

So I raised an extra-large flag, 15 feet by 25 feet on an 80-foot-high flagpole.

Watching that flag catch the wind and fly proudly was a beautiful sight. Except the city of Palm Beach decided my flag was too big. They claimed it exceeded zoning regulations. Who knew there was a law about the size of flag you are allowed to fly? When I politely informed them I had no intention of taking down my American flag, they began fining me $250 a day until I removed it.

As I said at the time, "The town council of Palm Beach should be ashamed of itself. They're fining me for putting up the American flag. The day you need a permit to put up an American flag, that will be a very sad day for this country."

My guess is you know what I did next. I filed a lawsuit against the town for $25 million, claiming my First, Eighth, and Fourteenth Amendment rights were being violated. As we wrote in that lawsuit, "A smaller flag and pole on Mar-a-Lago's property would be lost given the property's massive size, look silly instead of making a statement, and most importantly would fail to appropriately express the magnitude of Donald J. Trump's and the club members' patriotism."

Those fines added up to $120,000 by the time we had worked out a deal with the city. Rather than paying the fine, I donated $100,000 to Iraq War veterans' charities.

I actually thought that issue was done, but in 2014 the city of Rancho Palos Verdes, California, wanted me to lower the 70-foot-high flagpole flying over my golf course on the Pacific Ocean. One of the officials who wanted me to lower it admitted, "This flag now has become a symbol, and to the people in this community this flag symbolizes patriotism." So we won that fight!

As we all know, the flag is much more than a red, white, and blue cloth rectangle. It is a symbol to me, to you, and to people around the world. It represents equality, hope, and fairness. It represents great courage and sacrifice.

Everyone has heard me talking about our immigration problem. Well, there is an important reason that people are willing to risk their lives to get into this country. In 2015, more than 4.4 million people had applied and were waiting to legally emigrate to the United States—that list even includes more than 50,000 Iranians. For people coming from some countries, the estimated waiting period is 33 years. We also have somewhere between 12 and 15 million people here legally on green cards or temporary visas. Nobody knows how many illegal immigrants are here, but the usual estimate is more than 11 million people.

For the last several years I've been watching things change. Like most of you, I don't like what has been happening. I was asked by Chuck Todd on *Meet the Press* when the last time was that I thought America was living up to its promise. During the administration of Ronald Reagan, I said. It was a time when we felt so proud to be Americans.

I've spent my entire career standing up for this country. There is a writer on a conservative site who doesn't like me at all. I understand that—these people all have their favorite politicians. But even while he was calling me some nasty names he wrote, "And tell me: Why is Donald Trump . . . the only candidate willing to unambiguously state that the first duty of American politicians is to American citizens? Would those who disagree kindly provide us with a list of their priorities, showing us exactly where they think American citizens fall?"

I believe in always putting the interests of American citizens first—always. There aren't any second or third places. That level of commitment is what has been missing for so long in our foreign policy, in our trade policy, in our immigration policy. Somewhere we started worrying too much about what other countries thought about us. Does anybody reading this believe that I'm concerned about making other countries feel good? They used to fear us. They used to want to be us. We were respected.

Many years ago my daughter Ivanka went to what was then Czechoslovakia to visit her mother's family. At that time it was a Communist country. She told me that the Czechs would tape

American currency to the windshield of their cars, even if it was just a dollar bill, to show how proud they were to have anything from America. Even a one-dollar bill—they just wanted that association with America. Now? Now they're laughing at us. There's an old phrase that, sadly, you rarely hear anymore: "Made in America." We will start saying this again—in spades. We're unique. In case there's any doubt, that is exactly what I believe.

One way I have always shown my patriotism is by strongly supporting our military. We haven't been doing such a good job of that lately, but that needs to change. Our military must have all the manpower and the tools it needs to fulfill any mission. I like to say that the United States military should be so strong that we will never have to use it.

I was absolutely horrified to find out that we have been sending our soldiers into combat situations without the best available protection. It wasn't so long ago that parents were raising money at home to buy additional available protection and sending it to their kids in combat. I couldn't believe it. We need to make this promise to our fighting forces: No American will ever go into the field unless he or she has the best equipment available and as much of it as is needed. And when our troops come home, we are going to take good care of them. They are going to have the medical care they've earned. They are going to be respected for their service. The way we treat our veterans today is a disgrace, and that needs to change.

Unlike a lot of politicians, my active involvement with our veterans began more than two decades ago, when only about one hundred spectators turned out to watch New York's annual

Veterans Day parade. In that case this country was "celebrat-ing" the 50th anniversary of the end of World War II.

A hundred spectators? It was humiliating. It was an insult to those men and women who had literally saved the world for democracy. One hundred people.

Mayor Rudy Giuliani and I decided to do something about it. I donated a one-million-dollar matching grant to finance a second parade. On November 11, I walked down Fifth Avenue with 25,000 veterans, many of them dressed in their uniforms, as an estimated 1.4 million spectators cheered them. That was a parade worthy of their sacrifice, and one of N.Y.'s biggest ever.

A month later, I was honored at the Pentagon at a lunch at-tended by the secretary of defense and the entire Joint Chiefs of Staff. Since that time I've actively supported veterans' causes and hired veterans throughout my organization.

Currently the biggest crisis our veterans are facing is get-ting the medical care they were promised. We've got young men and women who come back from Iraq and Afghanistan and have to fight to get the treatment they need and were promised. We made a contract with all our veterans and we're not delivering. How in the world can we talk about how much we love this country when we're not taking care of the people who protect us? In September I said we need to take the exist-ing system apart. We need to create a whole new system. We have to, and it will really work.

The Department of Veterans Affairs (VA) is probably the most incompetently run agency in the United States govern-ment. And that's saying something. If it was one of my compa-nies, the people running it would have been fired a long time ago. The problem is that there are too many political people involved within its operation. It is astonishing that illegal immigrants in many cases are treated better than our veterans. The taxpayers pay more than $150 billion a year for the VA, and what do we get for that?

The *Las Vegas Review-Journal* summed it up correctly in 2014, saying, "The Department of Veterans Affairs finally is under intense scrutiny for its bogus waiting lists and the unconscionable treatment delays that have caused an untold number of preventable patient deaths. But new information shows that malfeasance, malpractice, and outright corruption within the VA is worse than Americans could have imagined— much worse."

That needs to end. Right now the VA is being run by people who don't know what they're doing. They're getting more money from the government than ever before and yet the care gets worse. The list of men and women waiting for care is growing and their wait times are longer. How can the VA possibly be so inefficient? We need to put people in charge who know how to run big operations. We have to get the best managers and give them the power, the money, and the tools to get the job done. We owe our veterans nothing less.

One way or another, we are going to take care of our veterans. If the VA hospitals can't do the job, then the veterans go to private doctors, private hospitals. The government will reimburse those doctors and those hospitals because we must fulfill our obligation to our veterans.

Finally, jobs: What kind of country sends their young men and women off to fight for them and then, when they come back, tells them, "Sorry, but while you were gone other people got all the jobs"?

Getting a good job is hard, but it's even more difficult for a veteran. Too many veterans find themselves struggling to find an opportunity. They have been out of the job market, often for several years. So we need a program that recognizes the sacrifices they made for all of us and puts them right back in the middle of the job market.

Being born in this country is a matter of luck. Being grateful and proud of this country and what it represents and honoring the people who have protected it is a privilege I am proud to share with all Americans.

11

★　★　★

THE RIGHT TO BEAR ARMS

THE SECOND AMENDMENT IS clear to me: "A well regulated Militia, being necessary to the security of a free State, the right of the people to keep and bear Arms, shall not be infringed."

Period.

The fact that the Founding Fathers made it the Second Amendment, second only to our First Amendment freedoms of speech, religion, the press, and the right of assembly and to petition the government, shows that they understood how important the right to bear arms would be for all Americans.

James Madison pointed out that this right was a unique historical protection when he said that the Constitution preserves "the advantage of being armed, which the Americans possess over the people of almost every other nation . . . [where] the governments are afraid to trust the people with arms."

We all enjoy this fundamental right in order to defend our-selves and our families. The Founding Fathers knew it was essential to a free society and passed this amendment to make sure the government could never take it (or our arms) away. Throughout history, we've seen oppressive governments consolidate and ensure their control over those they govern by taking away the means necessary for citizens to defend themselves.

I own guns. Fortunately, I have never had to use them, but, believe me, I feel a lot safer knowing that they are there.

I also have a concealed-carry permit that allows me to carry a concealed weapon.

I took the time and the effort to get that permit because the constitutional right to defend yourself doesn't stop at the end of your driveway. That doesn't apply just to me either. It applies to all our driveways or front doors.

That's why I'm very much in favor of making all concealed-carry permits valid in every state.

Every state has its own driving test that residents have to pass before becoming licensed to drive. Those tests are different in many states, but once a state licenses you to drive, every other state recognizes that license as valid.

If we can do that for driving—which is a privilege, not a right—then surely we can do that for concealed carry, which is a right, not a privilege. That seems logical to me.

The Second Amendment has been under attack for a long time. Throughout the years, state governments have chipped away at it, adding restrictions. No other right in the Bill of Rights has been attacked as often as the Second Amendment. Some of these restrictions obviously make sense. For example, felons and mentally ill people should not have access to guns.

A purpose of a gun among other things is to offer protection, to warn those people who would try to harm us that we are carrying a weapon and that we will use it.

In order to protect the Second Amendment, there are several significant steps we need to take. Most important, we need to start getting serious about prosecuting violent criminals. Sometimes it looks to me like the Obama administration has made only a token effort to take violent offenders off our streets.

The problem is compounded by the pressure being put on police departments by community organizations who seek to make our police do their jobs with one hand tied behind their backs.

Violent crime in our inner cities is out of control. Murder rates are way up. There are far too many hardened drug dealers and gang members who are repeatedly involved in burglaries and drive-by killings. We need to get them off the streets so that they don't continue to terrorize their neighborhoods and ruin more lives.

Here's an example of what can work. In 1997, a program called Project Exile was started in Richmond, Virginia. It mandated that if a criminal was caught committing a crime with a gun, he had to be tried in federal court rather than city or state court. If convicted, there was a mandatory minimum sentence of five years in a federal prison without a chance of parole or early release.

This was such a sensible program that it was supported by

both the NRA and the Brady Campaign, sponsors of the Brady Bill, which had fought for restricted gun ownership.

The Project Exile program was enacted and it worked. This message was posted on billboards around the city: "An Illegal Gun Gets You Five Years in Federal Prison." In the first year, homicides and armed robberies declined by about a third, and 350 armed criminals were taken off the streets.

A decade later, when the primary elements of the program had been supplemented by a somewhat less tough state law, the number of homicides in Richmond had still been cut by more than half.

Why is this important to law-abiding gun owners? First of all, it offers an intelligent approach to reducing crime, something we all want. Second, it clearly shows that guns are not the problem—dangerous, unstable criminals are the problem.

The antigun lobby still seems to be confused about this distinction.

We don't need to keep guns out of the hands of law-abiding citizens. We need to crack down harder on the career criminals who traffic in guns illegally. Programs like Project Exile will help make our communities safer.

Another important way to fight crime is to create an environment where our law enforcement officers are appreciated for all the good work they do as opposed to being singled out and criticized for the few bad officers who give police a bad name. I realize—and deeply regret—those situations where a police officer acted poorly under pressure and used unnecessary force.

These incidents always draw much more attention than the exemplary police work that goes on day-to-day.

Let's be clear about one thing: Our police do an amazing job in dealing with all the potentially explosive situations they face on a daily basis. We know, for example, that most crime is committed locally, within a neighborhood or even a household, where an argument can escalate into violent anger and action.

Who gets called into these situations? The police, of course. It is their job to rush in and calm things down. They are protecting neighborhood residents from the criminals in their midst. Detectives have to pick up the pieces when a robbery or murder occurs, so that the perpetrators of crimes can be brought to justice. Our law enforcement officers are very professional and well trained.

Ultimately, protecting ourselves and our families is our own responsibility. I know that. We have to be alert and report suspicious strangers or packages. We have to create community boards that can work in tandem, not in "gotcha mode," when dealing with local authorities. As relatives and friends, we have to be vigilant when someone close to us is suddenly showing deep signs of depression or erratic behavior while posting threats on social networks.

We also have the right to protect ourselves with gun ownership. It's as fundamental as choosing our type of religious worship or allowing the press to be critical of our government.

What is foolish and unnecessary is the media criticism that

immediately ties a well-publicized crime to the gun rather than to the criminal.

There are a number of steps that can be taken that will benefit all Americans, including the millions of law-abiding gun owners as well as those people who believe wrongly that guns are the source of our crime problems.

We have to keep guns out of the hands of people with mental health issues. The fact that people with mental health problems can obtain guns is not right. We all agree about that and we have to stop it, but there are some big hurdles.

Let's deal with reality: Our mental health system is broken, and it needs to be fixed. Politicians have ignored this issue because it is such a complex problem, and it might cost some big money.

But the fact is we need to fix this problem now.

Many of the mass murders that have taken place in this country over the last several years have one glaring fact in common: There were red flags that were ignored, and warning signs about the future "murderers" that were ignored. Parents and close friends, even Facebook friends, chose not to say anything or to look the other way. Denial is not responsible behavior.

Most people with mental health problems aren't violent; they just need help. We have to invest the money and resources to expand treatment programs that can provide that help. But there are people who are violent. They are a danger to the community and they are a danger to themselves.

There are people who should be institutionalized and not

My wonderful family.

CONFIRMATION CLASS
JUNE 1959
FIRST PRESBYTERIAN CHURCH
JAMAICA N.Y.

At my confirmation—First Presbyterian Church,
Jamaica, New York. I'm top row, second from the right.

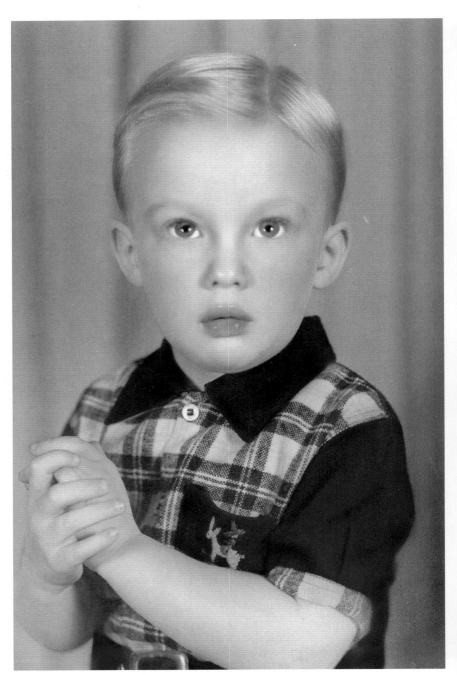

As a little boy.

My father and mother, Fred and Mary, at my graduation
from New York Military Academy.

Dancing with my daughter Tiffany at Mar-a-Lago.

With Ivanka, Don, and Eric.

Trump International Hotel on Pennsylvania Avenue in Washington DC, under construction. Formerly this was the Old Post Office.

The Trump Building at 40 Wall Street opposite
the New York Stock Exchange.

Trump Palace.

Trump International Hotel & Tower, One Central Park West.

Trump Tower, adjoining Tiffany's (whose air rights I purchased), between 56th Street and 57th Street on Fifth Avenue.

Trump International Hotel & Tower on the river in Chicago.

The Bank of America Building, San Francisco.

Trump World Tower—90 stories, opposite the United Nations.

With my sisters and brothers.
Left to right: Robert, Elizabeth, Fred Jr., me, and Maryanne.

Trump National Doral, Miami.

Trump Golf Links at Ferry Point.

Trump International Hotel in Las Vegas—Las Vegas's tallest building.

With President Ronald Reagan, a great guy, at the White House.

With my beautiful
wife, Melania.

At the office with Don,
Ivanka, and Eric.

living on the streets. Judges say they are entitled to their rights, which of course is true. They are entitled up to the point when they become dangerous to others and themselves. Then the situation changes. Then we have to protect the rights of young children going innocently to school or families out for a relaxing evening at a movie.

Why is this important to law-abiding gun owners? Because you are the citizens the antigun movement and the media blame when a deranged madman uses a gun to commit a horrific act. When one of these tragedies occurs, you can be sure two things are going to follow. First, opponents of gun rights will immediately exploit the situation to push their antigun agenda, and second, none of their proposed restrictions would have prevented the tragedy from taking place.

We need real solutions to solve real problems. We don't need advocates of useless gun restrictions taking advantage of emotional situations to push their agenda.

So how can we protect and extend the rights of law-abiding gun owners? We accomplish that by educating all Americans about the facts. For example, there has been a long and expensive campaign to find different ways to ban guns or gun hardware. In effect, just get rid of guns. That's the answer gun control advocates give.

This tactic is a road to nowhere.

Opponents of gun rights often use a lot of scary descriptive phrases when proposing legislative action against various types of weapons. Ban "assault weapons" they say, or "military-style weapons," or "high-capacity magazines."

Those all do sound a little ominous, until you understand what they are actually talking about are common, popular semiautomatic rifles and standard magazines that are owned and used by tens of millions of Americans.

I worry when our social-policy makers, looking for a "cause," pick on guns. The Supreme Court has made it clear that the government simply has no business and, in fact, no right to dictate to gun owners what types of firearms law-abiding Americans are allowed to own. Gun owners should be allowed to purchase the best type of weapon for their needs, whether it's for self-protection, sport shooting, or any other purpose.

There has been a lot of speculation about background checks, as if researching the background of everyone attempting to legally purchase a gun will somehow keep guns out of the hands of criminals. The national background-check system has been in place since 1998. Every time a gun is purchased from a federally licensed gun dealer, which is how the overwhelming majority of all gun purchases take place, they have to go through a federal background check.

Unfortunately, as expected, bringing more government regulation into the situation has accomplished very little. The main "benefit" has been to make it difficult for a law-abiding American to buy a gun. As study after study has proven, few criminals are stupid enough to try to pass a background check or have their names in any kind of system.

So they get their guns the same way bad guys have always gotten their guns—by stealing them or by buying them from an unlicensed source or getting them from family and friends.

This system is another example of federal regulation that

has turned into a complete failure. When the system was put in place, gun owners were promised it would be instant, accurate, and fair. That isn't what has happened at all.

One final caveat. We need to allow our military members to carry firearms on bases and at recruiting centers. As we have seen, our current policies leave our military members—and their families—defenseless on their own bases. They can be sitting ducks for one crazy person with a machine gun.

In the end, we must understand and appreciate why the right to keep and bear arms is so essential for law-abiding citizens. And we must recognize that the red tape proposed to infringe upon that right is a tremendous waste and possible danger to us all. My sons Donald and Eric are members of the NRA—and so am I—and proud of it!

12

★　★　★

OUR INFRASTRUCTURE
IS CRUMBLING

THERE ARE SOME THINGS so obvious that even Joe Biden can see them.

Take, for example, the state of our country's infrastructure. Vice President Biden once said, "If I blindfolded someone and took him at two o'clock in the morning into the airport in Hong Kong and said, 'Where do you think you are?' they'd say, 'This must be America. It's a modern airport.' But if I blindfolded you and took you to LaGuardia Airport in New York, you'd think, 'I must be in some third-world country.'"

The good news is that London Bridge isn't falling down. But that bridge, which is now located in Lake Havasu City, Arizona, may be the only bridge in America that isn't in danger of falling down.

Our airports, bridges, water tunnels, power grids, rail

systems—our nation's entire infrastructure—is crumbling, and we aren't doing anything about it. Former secretary of transportation Ray LaHood knows all about this and got it right when he said, "If we are going to have safe transportation systems in America, you have to invest in them. We haven't done that."

He described our way of dealing with this problem as the "limp along, go along" system. "There's no vision. No leadership in Washington to fix it, and they are trying to put Band-Aids and duct tape and other things on these fixes and they simply do not work."

This country's infrastructure is falling apart. According to engineers, one out of every nine bridges in this country is structurally deficient, approximately a quarter of them are already functionally obsolete, and almost a third of them have exceeded their design lives.

Some of these bridges have already collapsed. Barry LePatner, who wrote a book about this topic, said the following: "Since 1989 we've had more than 600 bridge failures in this country and . . . a large number of bridges in every state are really a danger to the traveling public."

Our infrastructure is terrible, and it's only getting worse and more expensive to fix. It's already costing the American people an estimated $200 billion a year in reduced productivity. That number is increasing annually. Instead of being at the office or in the factory getting work done, Americans waste countless hours every day sitting in traffic jams or waiting for stalled trains. We depend on our truckers to deliver the goods we need, and they end up wasting an unbelievable amount of time because our highway system is falling apart.

I used to think the traffic jams in New York were the worst anywhere in the country; they're not even close anymore. The problems are everywhere. Our roads are corroded with potholes. Our airports? Are you kidding me? A disgrace.

When Joe Biden sees it, you know it's bad.

If you land at LaGuardia, it feels like the wheels of the aircraft have come off.

I fly in from China or from Qatar, and it's as if I've come from a different world. It isn't just LaGuardia, which by the way is finally getting billions of dollars to rebuild; this is a coast-to-coast problem. Los Angeles International Airport is an entirely different kind of disaster.

Our power grid, the infrastructure for electricity that keeps everything operating, is way out-of-date. There is simply no way it will be able to meet our power needs in the future. Our high-speed Internet access is only 16th best in the world. When I travel internationally, I see magnificent places you wouldn't believe. I see properly maintained bridges, tunnels, and airports. I see great highways and unbelievably efficient power systems.

Then I come home and I get caught in traffic, and when the car moves, it bangs over potholes. It never seems to get better.

I wonder, Why can't we get these problems fixed? The answer is that the people we put in charge don't know how to fix them.

We're spending billions of dollars protecting countries that should be paying us to do the job yet we can't build roads in our own cities. We can't build schools in our own communities. I've been to China numerous times, and everywhere you look there are cranes reaching toward the sky. The Chinese build new cities over there in about 12 minutes, while we take years to get the permits to add a dormer window to our own homes.

The World Economic Forum ranks the US infrastructure as only the 12th best in the world, behind countries like Spain, the Netherlands, and the United Arab Emirates. Part of the reason is that we don't spend enough to fix, build, or maintain our "plant." Europe and China spend as much as 9 percent of their GDP on infrastructure projects. We spend 2.4 percent.

When you talk about building, you had better talk about Trump. There is no single builder in this country who has his name on as great a range of projects as I've constructed.

New York City wasted seven years trying to get a skating rink done. I did it in less than four months—and got it done under budget. There was a huge railroad yard overlooking the Hudson River that nobody could figure out how to develop. Drive by there now and you'll see thousands of magnificent apartments, all with the same name on the buildings—Trump.

Think about 40 Wall Street, one of the greatest buildings in New York City. For a brief time, along with the Chrysler Building, it was one of the two tallest buildings in the world. But it had fallen into disrepair. It was awful. They couldn't rent office space there.

I bought 40 Wall Street and completely redid it. Now it is a classic—and by the way, 100 percent rented and a very profitable building. My home in Palm Beach, Mar-a-Lago, was once the greatest mansion in the country, but its previous owner, the United States government, had let it deteriorate. Nobody had the vision to see what it could be once again. I restored it, rebuilt it, and now—go online and you can see what I've accomplished there. We brought the property back to the greatness it once was—and then made it better!

The same can be true of our country.

In Washington, DC, I'm converting the Old Post Office Building on Pennsylvania Avenue into one of the world's greatest hotels. I got the building from the General Services Administration (GSA). Many people wanted to buy it, but the GSA wanted to make sure whoever they sold it to had the ability to turn it into something special, so they sold it to me. I got it for four reasons. Number one—we're really good. Number two—we had a really great plan. Number three—we had a great financial statement. Number four—we're EXCELLENT, not just very good, at fulfilling or even exceeding our agreements. The GSA, who are true professionals, saw that from the beginning.

That's the way the country should be run.

Fixing our infrastructure will be one of the biggest projects this country has ever undertaken. There isn't going to be a second chance to get it right. Let me ask you, if your own house was falling down and you had to hire someone to fix it before it completely collapsed, who would you hire? A guy who tells you what he's planning to do, or a guy who has proven what he can do countless times before?

In America, our house is falling down. Numerous times I've developed project after project. I raise the money, solve endless problems, bring in the right people, and get it done. Those are four words politicians can't use: *I get it done*.

There isn't any doubt that we are going to have to find a way to deal with our infrastructure problems if we want to be the greatest economy in the world. Our economy requires movement, literally and figuratively, and we need the infrastructure that can support and promote that movement.

When you are getting ready to start the greatest long-term building project in American history, you'd better have the right person in charge. You need someone who has done it before and who isn't intimidated to take on that tremendous responsibility. You need someone who knows how to deal with unions and suppliers and, without any doubt, lawyers. I deal with them all each day, and I don't lose to them.

Different people might approach complex problems like this differently. There are people who look at a problem like this and shake their heads, thinking that it can't be done. There is a name for people like that: Governor. Then there are people who talk about the issue, throw around other people's money, and maybe even show you drawings. There's a name for those people too: Senator.

For me, fixing the country's infrastructure would be a major priority project. I was speaking to thousands of people in New Hampshire when a nice young man asked me what I thought about the project being planned to send humans to Mars.

"I think it's wonderful," I told him. "But I want to rebuild our infrastructure first on Earth, okay?" I mean, I don't understand how we can put a man on the moon but we can't fix the potholes on the way to O'Hare International Airport.

Where are our priorities?

Before we build bridges to Mars, let's make sure the bridges over the Mississippi River aren't going to fall down.

I love difficult challenges. Nobody responds better than I do when I'm told that something can't be done. What other people see as a terrible problem, I see as a great opportunity. There is nothing, absolutely nothing, that stimulates the economy better than construction.

A few years ago, Moody's, the financial investment agency, calculated that every $1 of federal money invested in improving the infrastructure for highways and public schools would generate $1.44 back to the economy. The Congressional Budget Office said that infrastructure investments have one of the strongest direct economic impacts.

You know why that is? Jobs.

These projects put people to work—not just the people doing the work but also the manufacturers, the suppliers, the designers, and, yes, even the lawyers. The Senate Budget Committee estimates that rebuilding America will create 13 million jobs.

Our economy needs more available jobs. I know what the unemployment rate supposedly is, but I also know there is no such thing as the Easter Bunny. Ask the construction unions and trade unions how many of their members are looking for jobs. Ask the unemployed electricians, plumbers, and masons how hard it is to find a good job.

If we do what we have to do correctly, we can create the biggest economic boom in this country since the New Deal when our vast infrastructure was first put into place. It's a no-brainer. It's so obvious that even the Democrats can figure it out.

The biggest questions are "How much is it going to cost?" and "Where is that money going to come from?" Financing a project is far too complex for most politicians to understand.

These projects require real-world dollars, not figures on paper. Experience is required to understand how to budget properly.

I think we can all agree, after watching our politicians waste our tax dollars, that the last thing we want to do is to put them in charge of a trillion-dollar rebuilding program.

When I build a project, I watch the money. At least some of it is coming directly out of my pocket—and if I do the job right, a lot more is going back into that same pocket. I know what things cost, I know where the money goes, I know who is doing a good job, and I know who is just phoning it in. Our government should, too.

On the federal level, this is going to be an expensive investment, no question about that. But in the long run it will more than pay for itself. It will stimulate our economy while it is being built and make it a lot easier to do business when it's done—and it can be done on time and under budget.

There are a lot of different ways to finance these projects. We need to put together a variety of sources to get it done. In some places there need to be bonds issued. The money is there—we just have to get it into place. The beauty of this is that every city and state has needs, which means that we can truly make this a national effort, controlled at the local level.

If we are serious about making America great again, this is where we have to start. Not only will repairing our infrastructure create jobs and stimulate the economy, it'll make it easier for us all to get home at the end of a long day. And in this case we can make America beautiful again.

13

* ★ * ★ * ★ *

VALUES

THE ONE QUESTION I get asked all the time is, "Mr. Trump, how do I get rich?"

What they are really asking me is, "How do I achieve happiness?"

Most people believe that once they're rich they'll automatically become happy. I'm not going to pretend that being rich doesn't offer a lot of wonderful opportunities, but it doesn't necessarily make you happy. I've learned that wealth and happiness are two completely different things.

I know the richest people in the world. Many of them are great negotiators and great businesspeople. But they're not necessarily nice people, nor are they the happiest people. They're rich, they're smart—I'd hire them to negotiate for me anytime, yet their personal lives may leave something to be desired.

The happiest people I know are those people who have great families and real values. I've seen it. I know it. People who have a loving spouse and have children they really love are happy people. Religion also plays a very large factor in happiness. People who have God in their lives receive a tremendous amount of joy and satisfaction from their faith.

Those who have watched me fire people on *The Apprentice*, who have read my bestselling books, or who have attended my Learning Annex seminars think they know me. Well, they know part of me—my business side. The professional part. I usually don't speak much about my personal life or my personal values or about how I came to be who I am today.

To begin with, my father and my mother were enormous influences on me. Fred Trump was a rich man, but he made sure his kids worked hard. Believe me, he didn't hand us anything—we had to work for what we got. He would drag me around with him while he collected small rents in tough sections of Brooklyn. It's not fun being a landlord. You have to be tough.

I'd see him ring the bell and then stand way over to the side of the door.

"How come you're over there?" I asked once.

"Because sometimes they shoot right through the door," he replied. Rent collectors usually did this work, but the methods were the same.

My work ethic came from my father. I don't know anybody who works harder than I do. I'm working all the time. It's not about money—I just don't know a different way of life, and I love it.

I raised my own kids the same way my parents raised me. I have five great kids. While my older ones were growing up, I'd have dinner with my kids almost every night. When they needed me, I was there for them.

Truthfully, I was a much better father than I was a husband, always working too much to be the husband my wives wanted me to be. I blame myself. I was making my mark in real estate and business, and it was very hard for a relationship to compete with that aspect of my life.

My kids were a different story. I was always there for them. My two oldest sons claim they're the only sons of a billionaire who know how to run a Caterpillar D10. While my daughter Ivanka's friends were vacationing in the South of France, she was in New York working.

My children have great mothers. My kids were raised to become hardworking, respectful adults. I could not be prouder of them. We never had any of the drug or alcohol problems that some of my friends' families have had to deal with. Hopefully it stays that way! Now I see my kids becoming great parents.

Growing up in Queens, I was a pretty tough kid. I wanted to be the toughest kid in the neighborhood and had a habit of mouthing off to everybody while backing down to no one. Honestly, I was a bit of a troublemaker. My parents finally took me out of school and sent me upstate to the New York Military Academy. I had my share of run-ins there as well.

While I wasn't afraid to fight, eventually I got the message. I learned respect for other people. I learned self-discipline. By the time I was a senior, I was made cadet captain—one of the highest ranking cadets.

My religious values were instilled in me by my mother. The first church I belonged to was the First Presbyterian Church in Jamaica, Queens. I went there every Sunday for Bible class. The church had a strong influence on me. Later I went to Reverend Norman Vincent Peale's Marble Collegiate Church when I was in New York, and joined Bethesda-by-the-Sea in Palm Beach, Florida.

Reverend Peale was the type of minister that I liked, and I liked him personally as well. I especially loved his sermons. He would instill a very positive feeling about God that also made me feel positive about myself. I would literally leave that church feeling like I could listen to another three sermons.

I learned a lot from Norman Vincent Peale, who wrote the classic *The Power of Positive Thinking*.

I think people are shocked when they find out that I am a Christian, that I am a religious person. They see me with all the surroundings of wealth so they sometimes don't associate that with being religious. That's not accurate. I go to church, I love God, and I love having a relationship with Him.

I've said it before—I think the Bible is the most important book ever written—not even close.

Perhaps *The Art of the Deal* is second. (Just kidding!)

I've had a good relationship with the church over the years—God is in my life every day. I don't get to church every Sunday, but I do go as often as I can. A lot of Sundays, when there's a special occasion, and always on the major holidays, I make sure I am there. People like to give me Bibles, which I love.

Jimmy Fallon asked me a question on his show one night:

"Have you ever apologized? Ever, in your whole life?" I told him that I think apologizing is a great thing—but you have to have been wrong. Then I promised, "I will apologize in the distant future if I am ever wrong." The audience laughed, as they should have. If you want to know if I've ever been wrong, the best thing to do would be to ask my kids. They'll tell you the truth about that.

Of course I've done things wrong. Show me a human being who hasn't. But when I do, I go out and try to make things right. I try to do a better job going forward.

I have been asked if I thought the Gospels would have a bearing on my public policy choices. That question has been asked of candidates for political office since Al Smith, a Catholic, ran for president in 1928. Many people thought JFK ended the discussion in 1960 when he said he would be president of all Americans. I am who I am, and deep down the Gospels helped make me that person. In business, I don't actively make decisions based on my religious beliefs, but those beliefs are there—big-time.

What does offend me is the way our religious beliefs are being treated in public. There are restrictions on what you can say and what you can't say, as well as what you can put up in a beautiful public area. The fact is that our deep-rooted religious beliefs have made this country great. That belief in the lessons of the Bible has had a lot to do with our growth and success.

That's our tradition, and for more than 200 years it has worked very well. For years you'd have beautiful mangers in public spaces and nobody complained about it.

Now? Mary and the baby Jesus are seldom shown. Even the word "Christmas" has somehow become controversial.

Who in the world could be offended by someone saying "Merry Christmas"?! That greeting isn't critical of any other religion, and it isn't being disrespectful to those who practice another religion. It's a wonderful tradition.

I don't understand why the same people who demand respect for their beliefs often don't show respect for the beliefs of others. It seems like every week there is a negative ruling on some issue having to do with Christianity. I think it's outrageous, totally outrageous. The president should do something about it. If the president has to go through the court system to do it, the president should do it. But this president won't.

It's well-known I am not fond of President Obama. I think he has been an awful president. His inexperience and arrogance have been very costly to this country. He's weakened our military, alienated our allies, and emboldened our enemies. He's abused his power by taking executive actions that he had no right to take. The next president is going to have to reverse and repeal many of the actions he's taken.

I did take a lot of criticism for not responding when an individual made what some people considered to be an anti-Muslim comment at an event in New Hampshire. People have their beliefs and their opinions. It's not my job to defend the president. President Obama would never defend me.

Anybody who wonders how I feel about women should just take a good look at the Trump Organization.

My positive feelings about women are reflected in the number of women who have worked in my organizations. I placed women in important leadership positions in the Trump Organization long before anybody else gave them that opportunity because I knew they could handle it. I was the first developer ever to put a woman in charge of a major construction project in New York City.

On *The Apprentice*, I was always pointing out the business skills of women. Talk to any of the women who worked for me and they will all tell you the same thing—I am a tough, demanding boss. I reward success and I penalize failure. I treat women no differently than I treat the men who work for me. I give women the responsibility they earn with their performance, I pay them the same, promote them accordingly, and, when they mess up, fire them the same.

I couldn't be more proud of my record with women.

Maybe my spokesperson on this subject should be my daughter Ivanka. I take a tremendous amount of pride in the fact that my children not only work with me, but when I'm criticized, they are the first to defend me.

14

* ★ * ★ * ★ *

A NEW GAME IN TOWN

CONTRARY TO THE JOKES, I don't think the White House needs any bright neon signs on the roof. No need to add additional wings or to sell the air rights.

I do, however, think we need to bring some business acumen to the White House.

The one thing you can be certain about is that, unlike the Obama administration, I stand up for this country, proudly and loudly. I continue to be exactly what I have been—the greatest cheerleader for America—the America that won rather than constantly lost.

As has become evident throughout my life, I am not afraid to look my opponents right in the eyes and say exactly what I believe.

I never worry about being politically correct. I don't need to read the polls to make my decisions.

And I don't see any reason to change my approach.

The issues facing our country are too important for anything less than an honest assessment of where we are and what needs to be done.

We are unique among the nations of the world, and we should be leading, not following.

Winning, not losing.

We have an amazing history. America is the greatest country that has ever existed on the Earth, and yet for some reason our leaders are reluctant to press our advantage.

I've successfully built one of the most respected brands in the world by representing it in everything that I do. I realized a long time ago that if I'm not proud of what I'm selling, then there is no reason for anybody else to feel that pride.

I put my own name on my buildings and on my products, and I stand behind them. People have come to expect top quality from anything that carries my name.

There is nothing in this world in which I take more pride than the United States of America. I will always be its best defender, and the best salesperson and cheerleader we've ever had.

America is the leader of the free world—we've earned the right to boast and make it clear that we are ready and willing to do whatever is necessary to defend this country as well as liberty anywhere in the world.

Our national anthem gets it right: This is the land of the free and the home of the brave. It's time we lived that message and let the world know we're willing to back it up.

Making America Great Again means standing by our word. We've watched President Obama draw a line in the sand, then another line in the sand, then no line at all. We've become an embarrassment to ourselves and to our history.

When your allies don't trust you and your enemies don't fear you, you have zero credibility in the world. Right now, our allies don't know what to believe about us, or how, or if, to value our word. President Obama has been talking into the wind for a long time.

We've seen Putin ignore him. We've seen just about every faction warring in Syria pay no attention to him. We've seen the Chinese taking tremendous advantage of our trade policies. We've seen the Iranians leave the conference table where we were negotiating a nuclear treaty (where a "new era" of cooperation is proclaimed), and then a few weeks later the Ayatollah is threatening again to destroy Israel—and laughing at the US.

Closer to home, only blocks away from the White House, Congress is preparing to decide whether or not to shut the government down. This happens almost every other year.

We need a leader who is going to restore the respect this country enjoyed in the past. I'm criticized for not issuing elaborate, detailed policy statements. What good are detailed plans if your country doesn't have the credibility to carry them out—but I issue them anyway.

Let's go back to the basics, back to the America our citizens embraced, because we were recognized as *the* major force for progress and peace.

Many of the lessons I've learned in business are applicable

to our current situation. The most important lesson is this—
Stand behind your word, and make sure your word stands up.
People who have done business with me will tell you that I
never say something unless I mean it.

I don't make promises I can't keep. I don't make threats
without following through. Don't ever make the mistake of
thinking you can bully me. My business partners and employees know that my word is as good as any contract—and that
better go for the other side's word as well.

I stand behind *my* commitments, and *our* commitments as
a nation.

I stand—without question—behind the Constitution at
home, and I stand, without question, behind our allies abroad.

No friendly country, and no allied leader, should question
our ironclad support again.

No enemy, and no enemy leader, should misinterpret our
resolve to fight to the death—their death.

We won't need the president of Israel to come to our shores
and explain to Congress what we used to stand for.

Making America Great Again means never taking another
step backward. Yes, we'll take inspiration from the heroism
of our past, but we're only going to charge ahead now. When
I played sports growing up, there was a saying in the locker
room: If you take the first step backward, you might as well
just keep going.

To put it another way: If you can accept losing, then you've
already lost.

There have been times in business when it has made sense

to change strategy or even walk away from a deal. You must never be afraid to walk away from a bad deal.

Someone should explain that principle to President Obama and John Kerry.

It's only by being willing to say "enough" that you gather strength and force your adversaries to modify their behavior.

I understand that you can't be totally rigid in negotiations. But on our core principles and core strengths, there can be no backing up or retreat. That's why we need to rebuild our military, so that no one will have any doubt about our strength or our intentions. If we are challenged, we will meet that challenge, and other leaders and other countries will think seriously before they doubt us again.

My own style of conducting business is straightforward. I think big. I aim very high, and then I keep pushing and pushing toward that goal—and beyond it. In the end I may not get everything I want—I understand that—but I never compromise on the basic goals I set out for.

Making America Great Again means convincing the smartest and the best people to come to Washington and join in putting our country first. The truth is that politicians have given government a bad name. It's a shame. The best people don't want to get involved in a bureaucracy where nothing ever seems to get done.

Who can blame them?

The kinds of people we need in government are executives who know how to get things done. These are the types of workers and executives who already are, or who will become, stars in any industry. There are also many workers in our civil service who are waiting for good leaders to inspire them.

Years ago these types of people wanted to be in government because they had faith that government was there to help people and that they could contribute to our nation by doing a good job. They believed in the service part of public service.

Now those inside the Washington circles are demoralized. Those outside don't want to go there. So many people go to Washington aiming to change it only to see themselves changed instead. And not for the better.

Ambitious government workers can't break through the red tape, and that drives them to leave government to go into private industry. You end up with mostly careerist "lifers" doing the day-to-day work.

It's a terrible cycle. The government is filled with good people who are stymied in trying to get things done, and because nothing gets done, the best people outside Washington don't want to go into government, so nothing ever gets done or improves.

We need to create an exciting atmosphere and put good people in the right position to Make America Great Again. One reason we rarely have difficulty recruiting the people we want for the Trump Organization is that they know they are going to play a key role in an aggressive company that exists to make big things happen. It is an exciting place to work.

People want to have a stake in that type of organization. They know they are going to be respected and judged on their accomplishments. They know that life in my company is never going to be boring and that they are going to be well rewarded for their hard work and share in the success.

Really talented outsiders will relish the thought of becoming part of the future. Of course, due to necessary budget controls, there will be fewer employees in the government overall. This just means the competition will be even fiercer to become one of the best.

Making America Great Again means restoring law and order, both on the street and in our courtrooms. Our police officers are doing an incredible job keeping us as safe as possible, but the job is getting harder for them because they aren't getting the support they need. Like our military, they must have whatever equipment they need to protect themselves and all our honest, hardworking citizens.

Government must be on their side instead of coddling criminals.

Obviously that means putting judges on the bench who will uphold the law rather than look for loopholes or try to make law.

We need to appoint justices—not just on the Supreme Court, but throughout the entire federal system—who will leave lawmaking to the legislators, as specified in the Constitution. The next president may well have the opportunity to appoint two or more Supreme Court justices. These appointments could determine the direction of the court for several decades. We need the right caliber of judge sitting in the highest courts.

Making America Great Again begins at home. It means restoring a sense of dignity to the White House, and to our country in general. The president of the United States is the most powerful person in the world. The president is the spokesperson for democracy and liberty. Isn't it time we brought back the pomp and circumstance, and the sense of awe for that office that we all once held?

That means everyone working in the administration should look and act professionally at all times—especially the president. The way you dress and the way you act is an important way of showing respect for the people you are representing and the people you are dealing with. Impressions matter.

Making America Great Again means taking our country back from the big-money interests. We have a country where the big problems can't be solved by consensus because the small-minded lobbyists and special interests are clogging the halls of Congress with their "special access."

Everyone talks about listening to the voice of the people. But how can you hear that voice when no one represents that voice? I am listening.

Let's restore trust and pride in our country by Making America Great Again.

15

★　　★　　★

TEACHING THE MEDIA
DOLLARS AND SENSE

"I HOPE DONALD TRUMP, the pompous host of *Celebrity Apprentice*, runs for president," wrote *Washington Post* columnist Michelle Singletary in April 2015. She continued: "Then we'll get a certified look at his income, investments, and debts. But here's a Trump-like prediction, which is like the various pronouncements made by the real estate developer that aren't backed by any credible evidence: Trump will not run. He won't officially declare his candidacy because the Ethics in Government Act requires those running for federal office to file disclosures of their personal finances."

Kyle Smith, resident genius at Rupert Murdoch's *New York Post*, also had it all figured out.

He wrote—"Big news coming from Donald Trump. Big, huge. I have the news before anyone else. Donald Trump is running for president . . . of the Donald Trump Love & Admiration Society. He's sure to be elected in a landslide. Oh, that other thing? Nah. No chance. When Trump declared to the Republican Party of Iowa's Lincoln Dinner that he is going to make an announcement in June 'that's going to surprise a lot of people,' he wasn't preparing to launch his long-awaited candidacy. He was simply doing what he always does: Promote the Donald. Generate headlines. Get people talking."

The truly odious Jonah Goldberg of the *National Review* was his usual incompetent self when he wrote—"Arguing with Trump is sort of like dressing up an adorable toddler in a Viking outfit and listening to him say he will raid my village and slaughter all in his path. It's cute. It's funny. Maybe it's even vaguely disturbing if he goes on too long . . . But, just as with Trump's ranting, the one thing you don't ever do is take it seriously."

This is the sad and often pathetic state of our "objective" media today. The people who are supposed to be reporting the news have no concept of fairness, because they believe themselves to be the experts. They "know better"—they have the inside scoop.

They never get embarrassed, but they should be. They must think their readers are idiots who forget how often they get it wrong. After I declared that I was running, a lot of them still didn't believe it.

Somehow they all "knew" that I wouldn't file the financial disclosures—because maybe Trump isn't as rich as people think he is. As it turned out, after the filing I was much richer.

As the "brilliant" Goldberg wrote (getting it completely

wrong again), "In the past, Trump always pulled back from the brink. Why risk his beloved TV show? Why endure the embarrassment of revealing he's not as rich as he claims . . . But something changed . . . And Trump took the leap—though he hasn't provided the required financial disclosures yet, which inclines me to think that he will either suddenly find an excuse to retreat or that he has a team of accountants trying to figure out how he can simultaneously save face and avoid perjury."

It's incredible to me how dishonest the media in this country really is. People sometimes forget that the newspapers and television stations are profit-making businesses—or at least they're trying to be. If they have to choose between honest reporting and making a profit, which choice do you think they will make?

The sad thing is that all it does is prove that both liberal and conservative news outlets can lie and distort the news shamelessly. I've had meetings with reporters who faithfully recorded what I said, then changed the words and the meaning.

Reporters have been writing about me and talking about me, even interviewing me, in newspapers, magazines, and on television for almost four decades. A lot of my press has been good and fair, but some of it has been incredibly dishonest and just terrible. I get along pretty well with a lot of the good reporters; it's those people trying to get attention by writing inaccurate stories about me and the Trump Organization that I really object to. There are some experiences I've never forgotten. I had a so-called journalist from a well-known publication come up to my office and interview me and several of my executives. We gave him a pile of paperwork, we gave him financial reports and statements, anything he asked for—then he wrote one of the most inaccurate stories I've ever read. The public pays attention to a story for less than a week, especially when you get as many stories as I do. But the impression a bad story leaves lasts a lot longer.

For a long time I had decided to ignore most of these attacks; I had buildings and golf clubs going up all over the world, my TV show was in the top ten, and I've got a great family. I didn't want to give them any more attention than they deserve. But then my cousin, John Walter, called and started complaining about a particular story he'd heard saying that I hadn't built a building since 1992 and told me I had to set the record straight. I couldn't continue to let reporters get it so wrong. I hadn't built a building since 1992? That's just bizarre. You'd have to be blind as well as ignorant to say something like that. It's got to be the easiest thing in the world to check the things I've accomplished. I'm bringing it up because it makes the point that you can't believe everything you read or hear—especially about someone like me.

I could list literally dozens of major projects I've done since 1992 (and I do in the appendix): But just for example, the award-winning 52-story Trump International Hotel and Tower opened in 1996. The 5-star Trump International Hotel and Tower opened in Chicago in 2009. The $1.3 billion Trump International Hotel in Las Vegas opened in 2008. The completely renovated "Crown Jewel of Wall Street," 40 Wall Street, which for a brief time was the tallest building in the world, reopened in 1996 and is totally rented. The renovated 555 California Street, the second-tallest building in San Francisco, reopened in 1996. The list goes on for pages. The 35-story Trump Park Avenue. Trump World Tower. I've built the best golf courses in the world, everywhere from Palm Beach to Aberdeen, Scotland. The Trump National Doral, Miami. I have three iconic golf courses in Scotland and Ireland with many hundreds of hotel and residential units that have been built or restored by me better than they originally were. I haven't even slowed down. The beautiful Old Post Office building in Washington, DC, will soon be the Trump International Hotel, Washington DC. I won a fierce bidding war for the opportunity to renovate this magnificent building, which is due to open in 2016. And many, many more. I've obviously been an extremely busy man since 1992!

So terrible, lazy reporting does bother me. I think it would bother anyone who works as hard as I do, and the amazing people who work for the company, when a reporter writes something that inaccurate. The next time you read or hear something about me that doesn't seem right, take a good look at the person who wrote it or said it on TV and see if you respect them.

Another reporter wrote in a major publication that my father gave me $200 million when I started out. Don't I wish! This reporter didn't even give me the courtesy of calling me to ask if that was true. He read it in an old book that had it wrong and wrote about it. There is no man in the world I loved or respected more than my father. He was my best friend and my mentor. He gave me his knowledge, his work ethic, and his drive to succeed. He built his own wonderful company in Queens and Brooklyn from nothing. But we worked in different times, on a different scale. He built good housing, and I've built major buildings and resorts in New York City and around the world. I took what I learned from my father and built my own business—and no one was more proud of me for doing it than my father. He told a business magazine once, "Everything Donald touches turns to gold!"

I'm proud of what I've built, so when so-called journalists get it wrong, I have to respond.

The problem is that it's getting worse. I know that every poll shows that the public doesn't trust the media. The irony about that is that the media is conducting those polls.

Even they have to admit people don't trust them.

Maybe the journalists' most embarrassing moment so far came when I filed my financial statement. I am the richest presidential candidate in history. I'm the only billionaire ever to run. I'm not accepting donations from my rich friends, special interests, or lobbyists. When was the last time someone running for political office didn't take money? The voters know it—and love it.

So maybe I shouldn't have been surprised at the response when I filed my 92-page-long financial-disclosure forms. My net worth is in excess of $10 billion—even more than people thought.

As any accountant will tell you, it's actually almost impossible to put down a specific number because large assets are always in flux. The total value not only changes every day—it changes every *hour*.

I also have significant foreign investments that are difficult to value. Plus, the forms we had to fill out weren't designed for someone like me. There were many places on the form where the only box I could check was "$50,000,000 or more." For example, one of my buildings is worth about $1.5 billion, but on the forms it is valued at only "$50,000,000 or more."

We checked off a lot of boxes. Wherever possible, we were accurate to the dollar.

I am never shy about creating news by being controversial and fighting back. Remember, we need to make sure this country stands up and fights back.

I've held more well-attended news conferences in the past few months than any other candidate. I always draw a large crowd of journalists who are like sharks, hoping I'll put some blood in the water.

I try to oblige.

I participated in the first Republican debate, and Fox drew the biggest audience for a news event in their history. In the second debate, CNN had the biggest audience in its history. I wonder how many people would have watched if I wasn't involved. Not many!

16

★ ★ ★

A TAX CODE THAT WORKS

THE ONE THING THAT everybody agrees about is that our tax system doesn't work. The current code is crazy. The federal tax code is 74,608 pages long. Nobody can really understand it, not even the accountants who try to help taxpayers fill out their forms. An entire industry springs up every year just to help Americans figure out how much money they owe to the government.

The reality is that the current tax code takes too much money from the people who need it most, while allowing others to find ways to reduce their tax burden. It discourages major corporations from reinvesting foreign profits here at home and makes it hard for small businesses to grow. It absolutely destroys jobs rather than helping create them.

A sensible tax plan would provide tax relief for middle-class

Americans, allowing hardworking people to keep more of their own money; it would reduce the taxpayers' annual anxiety and frustration by simplifying the whole tax code; it would grow the economy and create jobs by discouraging corporate inversions and make America competitive around the world; and it wouldn't add to either our debt or deficit.

The tax reforms I'm proposing address all those problems by simplifying the tax code for everybody: My goal is to put H&R Block out of business.

I described these solutions in an op-ed piece that appeared in the *Wall Street Journal* in late September 2015: "Tax Reform for Security and Prosperity," it was called.

I wrote that the top priority for the government of the United States should be to provide security for its people. That security includes removing uncertainty and making sure that the economic future of the country is assured through better deals, smarter trade agreements, and tax policies that unburden the middle class and unleash the private sector.

My approach to tax policy will do just what needs to be done. For all Americans the uncertainty and complexity of a tax code written for special interests and the very rich will be removed and a clear future will be available for all.

The plan has several goals. Let me make it clear that this set of policies takes dead aim at eliminating deductions and loopholes available to special interests and the very rich, as well as those deductions made redundant or unnecessary by the much lower tax rates every person and business will be paying.

In particular, I am proposing ending the current treatment

of carried interest for hedge funds and other speculative part-nerships that do not grow businesses or create jobs.

The first goal of the plan will be to provide tax relief. If you are single and earning less than $25,000 or married and earn-ing less than $50,000, you will not owe any income tax. This will immediately remove some nearly 75 million households from the income tax rolls.

Second, the tax code will be simplified. Instead of multiple tax brackets with multiple variations, there will be only four brackets: 0%, 10%, 20%, and 25%. This new code eliminates the marriage penalty and the Alternative Minimum Tax while providing the lowest tax rates since before World War II. Fur-ther, this plan eliminates the death tax, thus allowing families to keep what has been earned.

The proposed policies will allow the middle class to keep most of their deductions while eliminating many of the de-ductions for the very rich. With more money in middle-class pockets, consumer spending will increase, college savings will grow, and personal debt will decline.

Third, we need to grow the American economy. For the past seven years our economy has been at a virtual standstill. Growth in the Gross Domestic Product of less than 2 percent per year is pathetic. We need to spur production, bring home jobs, and make it easier to invest in America.

The plan states that any business of any size will pay no more than 15 percent of their business income in taxes. This low rate will make corporate inversions unnecessary and will make America one of the most competitive markets in the world. This plan will also require companies with off-shore

capital to bring that money back to the United States at a repatriation rate of only 10 percent. Right now that money is not
being brought back because the tax rate is so high.

Finally, this plan will not add to our deficits or our national
debt. With disciplined budget management and elimination of
waste, fraud, and abuse, this plan will allow us to balance the
budget, grow the economy at record levels, clear the backlog of
workers sitting at home, and begin the process of reducing our
debt. With moderate growth, this plan will be revenue neutral.
These changes will ensure huge economic growth, and this
country will be on the road to extraordinary prosperity.

This tax policy has the economic well-being of the country
and its citizens at the forefront. This plan is bold, but it is also
cast in reality and common sense. Growing the economy will
provide the security we need to make America great again.

While my op-ed summed it up, there are other important
points to make: When the income tax was first introduced,
only one percent of Americans were taxed. It was never intended to be a tax on most Americans. Under this plan the
income tax will be eliminated for nearly 75 million households,
and 42 million households that now have to file complex forms
that they often need expert advice just to figure out they don't
owe anything will file a one-page form that will save them
time, anxiety, frustration—and more than an average of $100
in preparation costs. More than 31 million households will also
use the simplified form—and they get to keep almost $1,000 of
the money they have worked for.

The great reduction in rates will make a lot of the current
exemptions and deductions—part of the reason the forms are

so complicated—unnecessary and redundant. But the deductions for charitable donations and on mortgage interest won't be touched. Those deductions have been very successful in accomplishing their objectives—assisting America's charities and helping people own their own homes. It also eliminates the death tax, because you earned that money and already paid taxes on it. You saved it for your family. The government already took its bite; it isn't entitled to more of it.

Our current tax code actually discourages business growth and penalizes success. Too many companies, from our biggest brands to innovative start-ups, are moving their headquarters out of the country, either directly or through corporate inversions. In an inversion a company moves its legal headquarters to a lower-tax nation and pays taxes there. It isn't illegal or dishonest or even unpatriotic, it's just good business. Any business that does not take advantage of the opportunity to increase revenue by lowering its taxes isn't being properly managed. The Democrats want to make inversions illegal, but that isn't going to work. Whatever laws they pass, with literally billions of dollars at stake, corporations will find methods to get around them. It makes a lot more sense to create an environment that welcomes business.

Under Ronald Reagan we had the best corporate tax rate in the industrialized world. Now we've got the worst. Rather than working with our corporations to rebuild our economy and create millions of jobs, we're practically forcing them to relocate. This tax plan would cut the corporate tax rate to 15 percent—for our small businesses and freelancers as well as the big corporations. Small businesses are the true engine of our economy.

According to the Council of Economic Advisors, American small businesses create 60 percent of our new jobs. But when tax credits and deductions are included, most small businesses are actually taxed at a higher rate than large corporations. Under existing tax law, sole proprietors, freelancers, unincorporated small businesses, and pass-through entities are taxed at the higher personal income tax rates. In reality, they are often taxed at twice the rate corporations actually pay. With the Internet changing the structure of the business world and encouraging start-ups, there are more of these than ever before. This is where our economic future is being built, where every dollar counts, and our tax code makes it tough for them to survive.

As long as these businesses are unfairly taxed at personal income rates, they will be at a huge disadvantage. The right plan would create a new 15 percent business tax rate within the personal income tax code that would substantially reduce taxes and help these businesses succeed and grow.

As you read this, American-owned corporations have as much as $2.5 trillion in cash sitting overseas. Just imagine what would happen if our corporations brought that money home. How many jobs would be created? Currently, they don't bring it home because the tax rate here is much higher than they are paying in other countries. A key component of this plan is a onetime repatriation of corporate cash now held overseas at a 10 percent tax rate. Under this plan, corporations would profit tremendously by bringing home that $2.5 trillion and putting it to work—while benefitting from the globally competitive, newly lowered corporate rate.

The big question everybody will ask is, How do you pay

for this wonderful plan? The good news is that it is revenue neutral—and that's before the economic growth that will be triggered by putting more money in your pocket and by the new jobs that will be created. This plan will be paid for by reducing or eliminating most of the deductions and loopholes that allow the very rich to pay lower taxes, by the repatriation of corporate cash held overseas, by putting an end to allowing corporations to defer taxes on income earned outside this country, and by cutting down or eliminating those corporate loopholes catering to special interests—in addition to those deductions that are made redundant or unnecessary by lowering the tax rate on corporations and business income. A reasonable rate of the deductibility of business interest expenses will also be phased in.

We also must finally reduce waste. Billions and billions of dollars are wasted annually, and nobody seems accountable. All politicians in every election cycle promise to reduce waste in spending. When was the last time you heard of government actually doing that? I'll answer that: Never. In business you learn that small savings very quickly become large savings. When you're spending your own money, you learn how to eliminate waste. The next president has to stop throwing your money away. Save a few billion here, a few billion there, and before you know it, you've made a real dent in spending.

This waste isn't difficult to find. In 2013, *Business Insider's* Walter Hickey went through the reports of each government agency's Inspector General and pretty easily identified $15 billion in quick savings, ranging from the $42 million given to a college by the Department of Education—that was ineligible to receive any federal funds, to the $2.7 billion that the Department of Health and Human Services could save just by reexamining the price that Medicaid and Medicare should pay for wholesale prescription drugs.

In 2015, the Citizens Against Government Waste issued its Prime Cuts report, showing how $648 billion could be cut from the 2016 budget without causing harm. $9.6 billion could be saved by ending the Rural Utilities Service program that makes loans and grants to utilities in underserved parts of the country—in one rural Arkansas town the government spent $5,500 per resident of your tax dollars to provide broadband access. It also points out the cost of a lack of supervision of different programs, noting that there are 6.5 million active social security accounts issued to people that supposedly are 112 years old or older—although there were only 35 known people of that age. And a lot of people have estimated that there is more than $100 billion in waste in the Medicare program.

The point is that we throw away billions of dollars every single year, and the next president has to finally do something to stop it.

It's time we finally brought our tax system up to date by reducing the burden on most Americans, simplifying the system for everyone, providing a sensible policy for large corporations and small businesses, and cutting out the billions of your dollars we waste every year . . . and then, to top it all off, bring our jobs back home where they belong.

17

*   *   *

MAKING AMERICA GREAT AGAIN

I WAS TWENTY-EIGHT YEARS old in 1974 when I got involved with my first major construction project. The once great Commodore Hotel, located right next to Grand Central Station, was a total mess. There had been a time when the Commodore was one of the greatest hotels in the world, but the hotel and the whole neighborhood had become run-down.

A lot of the buildings in the area were already in foreclosure, and many of the stores were boarded up. The exterior of the Commodore was filthy, and the inside was so dark and dingy that it felt like the building was on the verge of becoming a welfare hotel.

It was a dying building, in a dying neighborhood, in a struggling city.

I probably was still too young to know better. But you know what—I was the same person then that I am today, up for any challenge. I had total confidence in my ability to get great things done. But today I have the added benefit of truly great experience.

When I looked at the Commodore, I saw its potential—it would be the largest hotel renovation in New York City during the latter part of the twentieth century.

The neighborhood still had possibilities as well. Right in the heart of the Grand Central area, there were thousands of people walking by the hotel every day. I didn't have enough money to finance the deal myself, and I might not have risked it even if I had the money to do so.

All kinds of very smart real estate investors told me it wouldn't work.

And yet I had a vision of what could be done, so I never gave up. My enthusiasm and meticulous planning brought others to the table. I'm an unstoppable force when I'm excited, and I was in full Trump mode on this project—and many others since then.

During the years it took me to put this deal together, I learned a lot about working with the city and the banks, the construction industry and the unions. I could have just refurbished the existing structure, but that's not the way I think.

There were detractors all along the way. For instance, the preservationists were angry about my creating a new and beautiful glass exterior façade. Inside, I gutted all of the floors and replaced them with the best available materials.

The hotel, the Grand Hyatt, has been successful since the day it opened in 1980. It became the foundation for the restoration of the entire Grand Central neighborhood as well as my calling card—introducing the Trump quality brand to the people of New York.

That project marked the first time I took a large-scale failing property and made it great again. As part of that deal I fixed up the great Grand Central Terminal itself—it looked beautiful and clean again. I've done it over and over again in the thirty-five years since—and now for the really big and important one: our country.

★

We can take a crippled country and make it great again. Our country has been allowed to languish and become a tarnished, second-class place in the eyes of the world.

The challenges ahead are many. The naysayers from the media and the political establishment are out there because they fear any changes to the status quo from which they benefit.

But guess what? I have a vision and I understand the process by which we're going to accomplish our goals. We need to strengthen our military, help our vets, stand up to our enemies, deter illegal immigration, rebuild our infrastructure, revamp our tax code and educational system, and rip apart the ridiculous policies of the past, including Obamacare and the Iran nuclear "agreement."

Most important, we need to reinvigorate the American

dream and give our country back to the millions of people who have labored so hard for so little. Too many Americans are wondering (and who can blame them) what happened to this nation's great promise and the idea that each generation makes things better for their children.

Don't bet against what I am saying—I understand odds very well—because I've always tackled the hardest challenges and come out on top. My name has become one of the greatest brands in the world. I know how to win. I like what Jay Leno said at the ceremony to unveil my star on the Hollywood Walk of Fame. "It is now official," he proclaimed. "There is no place in America that doesn't have the Trump name on it."

Candidates for political office always say they're running on their record. Unfortunately, their records are made up of them talking about what they're going to do, rather than them getting things done.

Our nation's capital has become the center of gridlock. It seems like these days most of the energy in Washington is being spent deciding whether we're going to keep the government operating or not. No surprise there: Washington's been running a going-out-of-business sale for a long time.

It's no wonder that our president and Congress have such low ratings in the polls. No wonder that we've lost our influence and the basic respect of both our allies and enemies throughout the world.

Meanwhile, the Supreme Court has decided in their infinite wisdom to fill the breach by making social policy rather than defending our most precious historic assets, the US Constitution and the Bill of Rights.

We have three branches of government, but the trunk of that tree is rotting away.

For years I had thought about—but resisted—running for the presidency. Friends, colleagues, and customers encouraged me to do something. I thought, "I'm not a politician, and I have a huge, successful business to run."

But then I realized I couldn't stand what I was seeing. I couldn't believe the hypocrisy and inaction of Washington "insiders" who wanted to keep the gravy train flowing in their direction, while outside the Beltway, Americans were suffering and they were rightfully angry about the lack of leadership and creativity.

So when I spoke up, the media squawked, the politicians cringed, and the special interests realized that their days of influence were numbered.

A lot of people tried very hard to paint a bleak picture of what would happen.

Then the American people spoke.

The crowds started coming to my rallies in droves. We had to move our rallies into football stadiums and basketball arenas, while my competitors could barely fill small rooms. The national debates drew huge audiences—more than 24 million viewers—because our citizens felt hopeful again and wanted to hear what I had to say. And what I have been saying is that it is time to do everything necessary to Make America Great Again.

It begins by creating millions of good jobs for hardworking Americans. The Economic Policy Institute estimates we've lost more than five million jobs since 1997 because of the terrible trade deals we've made. Those jobs are coming back home. We've created too many jobs—in other countries.

Our military must be by far the greatest in the world, so when we negotiate deals with countries like Iran, we do it from strength. And when our soldiers come home, they must receive the care they have earned. This is the one national debt we should be thrilled to pay.

A great wall on our southern border must be built. It needs beautiful doors in it to welcome LEGAL immigration, but the flood of illegal immigrants must end. And we need to legally stop the practice of birthright citizenship; the Fourteenth Amendment was never intended to create a technical path to citizenship. Most Native Americans, for example, although they were born here, were not automatically granted citizenship—and it took almost 150 years before a law was passed making them citizens if they wanted to be.

And the Second Amendment was created to make sure Americans could protect themselves from tyranny. There is no way we will change it.

A revised revenue-neutral tax code—which conservative writer and commentator Wayne Root described as "close to perfect"—will put money back in the pockets of the people who need it most; and when you spend it—instead of the government—you'll be creating American jobs. It will encourage corporations to spend their earnings here, resulting in even more new jobs.

Our educational system needs to better prepare our children and retrain adults to succeed in the new digital marketplace. No one knows how to do that better than local communities. The federal government should not be telling local schools how to educate our children. Common Core will be dead.

Obamacare needs to be repealed and replaced with a sensible health care system that creates a competitive marketplace, which will reduce costs while providing for the medical needs of all Americans.

We can create tens of thousands of new jobs by rebuilding our collapsing infrastructure. These are the real shovel-ready projects: Roads, bridges, tunnels, and tracks have to be replaced or repaired before they crumble, and this will also put many thousands of people to work.

The most powerful people in Washington are lobbyists and special interest groups, whose money funds most elections and buys them influence. That has to stop, and electing someone who doesn't take their donations is a good first step.

We must have a viable energy policy that uses our abundance of resources to power America back to economic prosperity.

You can believe what I say, because to see what I've accomplished, all you need to do is take a nice walk through the greatest cities of the world—and look up. Look up, and you'll see the Trump buildings rising skyward.

I've done things that nobody else has done. The 68-story Trump Tower, on Fifth Avenue right next to Tiffany's, was the tallest entirely glass-exteriored building in Manhattan when it opened in 1983. That helped pioneer the modern luxury-building industry.

One of the things I'm most proud of about that building is

that the person I put in charge of overseeing construction was a 33-year-old woman. I made that decision in 1983, when the fight for gender equality in business was really beginning.

None of the people who whine about the way I talk to women mention the fact that I voluntarily promoted gender equality in a male-dominated industry. The women who work and have worked for me will vouch for the fact that I was as demanding of them as I was of their male counterparts.

That's the kind of "gender equality" we need: Leadership that inspires the best in people, male or female, not a wishy-washy former secretary of state who doesn't understand the lunacy of having her own private e-mail server.

Laying off thousands of workers and leaving companies in a mess is also not an accomplishment, at least not one to be proud of or to pretend qualifies you to run our country.

I always think big. I start with a plan to build the biggest, the most beautiful, and the highest-quality projects. If you don't begin with big dreams, you can never fulfill them. Trump buildings are all over New York, from 40 Wall Street to the West Side Railway Yards. From Columbus Circle to the Trump Palace on the East Side, and downtown to the SoHo Condominiums.

That's just for starters.

Eventually, we started building outside the city, and currently the Trump name is on buildings in nine states, from New York to Hawaii, from Florida to Washington, and in ten other countries, from Uruguay to India. Many large-scale and even massive projects are in the pipeline and ready to roll.

At 52 stories tall, 555 California Street is the second-tallest building in San Francisco, and the largest in terms of usable floor space. Originally the Bank of America's world headquarters, that building has been used in films, including *Dirty Harry* and *The Towering Inferno*.

It would certainly make anyone's day to be in it.

Trump World Seoul consists of six condominium buildings throughout Seoul and its neighboring cities. The glass-clad Trump Tower at Century City, featuring 220 condos, is one of the tallest buildings in Manila, Philippines.

The 72-story Trump Ocean Club in Panama City is Panama's first five-star development. We're building luxury hotels and residences all over the world. We're representing the best of America throughout the world with some of our best hotels and projects ready to be announced.

I understand "foreign policy" from the practical standpoint: I know how to make deals, bring foreign governments to the table, and negotiate deals that don't give everything away. In fact, the Chinese have their biggest bank in Trump Tower. They want to be part of Trump wherever they can.

That's why when I hear politicians talking about some trade bill they voted for or how they balanced the budget, I really have to laugh. Maybe they have political experience, but they certainly don't have common sense or real-world experience.

Every construction project, every deal, is totally unique. Each project is an unbelievable balancing act; I have to bring together the business community, the financial community, and the local officials. I've learned to work with great architects and designers. I've worked out deals with the unions and the trades.

I care about every detail. I read the small print, unlike the negotiators of the Iran nuclear "agreement," who don't seem to know what's in the "side deals," which Iran struck with the agency that is supposed to be responsible for verifying Iran's compliance.

When it came time to expand, I got interested in golf resorts. When I was a kid, my father would take me golfing with him. He didn't play much, but he had a beautiful swing. I looked around, and who did I see on the golf courses? Successful people; great businesspeople.

What were they doing as they played? They were talking about deals. I couldn't begin to guess how many great deals were made on a golf course. So I decided to build the best golf courses and resorts in the world, and that's what we've done.

People think it's hard to create a building? Try putting in a new golf course in New York City. In 2015 we opened Trump Golf Links at Ferry Point in the Bronx, and it instantly became one of the greatest public golf courses in the world. It's the first public golf course opened in New York in over half a century.

It was under construction for many years—a real mess.

Nobody else could get it done. People were running in the other direction. Nobody wanted to take on this project's completion.

The city had wanted a golf course built for decades, but nobody could figure out how to do it. After the politicians had screwed up this deal for many years, they brought in a businessman, me, to clean up their mess.

I created a magnificent golf course.

It's been a huge success for the city and for the Trump Organization. I promised that golfers would come from all over the world to play a round of golf in the Bronx, and that's exactly what has happened.

I don't just want to bring golfers to America. We need to bring all kinds of businesses back to America, especially those that are American-owned.

If we create the proper tax climate and cut the endless red tape restricting American businesses large and small, then we'll have a real job resurgence, which will help to create "full employment."

Full employment means we don't have 20 percent of the population either out of work or underemployed. Full employment means that every new worker can feel good about going home to his or her family with the pride of having done a hard day's work.

Full employment benefits unions and employers; together they can rebuild our country's infrastructure.

Full employment means that people who are now mortgaged beyond their means can get out from under the oppressive burden of worrying if their homes are secure. As credit loosens up from banks, the new and renovated housing industries will boom as well.

We are at a critical turning point in our history, not only for you and me but for our children as well. America may be struggling, it may be crippled, but we can rise again. Our time has not passed, it is here, and the potential is amazing.

America's best days are still to come. Why? Because of our people. Together we can Make America Great Again.

ACKNOWLEDGMENTS

I would like to thank David Fisher, Bill Zanker, Corey Lewandowski, David Cohen, Rhona Graff, Meredith McIver, Hope Hicks, and Amanda Miller for their enthusiasm and assistance throughout the writing of this book. Additionally, Byrd Leavell and Scott Waxman at Waxman Leavell Literary Agency, Don McGahn, and Carolyn Reidy, Louise Burke, Mitchell Ivers, Jeremie Ruby-Strauss, Irene Kheradi, Lisa Litwack, John Paul Jones, Al Madocs, Jaime Putorti, Jennifer Robinson, Jean Anne Rose, and Nina Cordes at Simon & Schuster brought their expertise to the table and delivered a finished product in record time. Thanks to all for your hard work—it is very much appreciated.

MY PERSONAL FINANCIALS

My net worth has increased since I released (at my presidential announcement) the attached financial statement which is dated as of June 2014. The value of my real estate in New York, San Francisco, Miami, Washington, DC, Europe, and many other places has gone up considerably. I have very little debt, and even that is at low interest rates. My current net worth is more than ten billion dollars.

My income for 2014, as I reported in the PFD statement, was $362 million dollars—not including dividends, interest, capital gains, rents, and royalties. Income for 2015 will exceed $600 million. I also did well in the stock market. While that isn't something that I've focused on in the past, and is only a small part of my net worth, 40 of the 45 stocks I bought rose substantially in a short period of time, resulting in a $27,021,471 gain on sale—the stocks remaining in the portfolio have an unrealized gain of more than $22 million.

On the financial disclosure forms I included more than 500 business entities, 91 percent of which I own completely. I also included the royalties from my book *The Art of the Deal*, one of the bestselling business books of all time, which is still selling after three decades, as well as my many other bestsellers.

I also reported receipts from my TV show, *The Apprentice*. NBC/Universal announced it was being renewed, and they were very disappointed when I informed them that I would not be available to be in the boardroom for our fifteenth season because of my run for president. They tried to talk me into it, but eventually hired Arnold Schwarzenegger—who will do a great job—to sit in my chair. During the 14 seasons of *The Apprentice* and *Celebrity Apprentice*, which is now being broadcast around the world, I made $213,606,575.

I was very pleased to file this disclosure and proud of what I've accomplished.

Donald J. Trump
Summary of Net Worth
As of June 30, 2014

ASSETS

Cash & Marketable Securities - as reflected herein is after $ 302,300,000
the acquisition and development of numerous assets
(i.e. multiple aircraft, land, golf courses and resorts, etc.),
the paying off of significant mortgages for cash and before
the collection of significant receivables.

Real & Operating Properties owned 100% by Donald J. Trump
through various entities controlled by him:
    Commercial Properties (New York City)   1,697,370,000

    Residential Properties (New York City)   334,550,000

    Club facilities & related real estate   2,009,300,000

    Properties under Development   301,500,000

Real Properties owned less than 100% by Donald J. Trump
    1290 Avenue of the Americas - New York City
    Bank of America Building - San Francisco, California
    Trump International Hotel & Tower - Las Vegas
    Starrett City - Brooklyn, NY
        Total Value Net of Debt   943,100,000

Real Estate Licensing Deals, Brand and Branded Developments   3,320,020,000

Miss Universe, Miss USA and Miss Teen USA Pageants   14,800,000

Other Assets (net of debt)   317,360,000
        Total Assets $ 9,240,300,000

LIABILITIES

Accounts payable $ 17,000,000

Loans and mortgages payable on Real and Operating
Properties owned 100% by Donald J. Trump
    Commercial Properties (New York City)   312,630,000

    Residential Properties (New York City)   19,420,000

    Club facilities   146,570,000

    Property under development   7,140,000
        Total Liabilities   502,760,000

    NET WORTH $ 8,737,540,000

Various Charitable Contributions
Over his lifetime, Mr. Trump has been a major contributor to both
charitable organizations and organizations dedicated to the
preservation of open space for the public's use, by donating
valuable parcels of land throughout the country. Over the last five
years, in excess of $102,000,000 has been contributed for such
purposes by Mr. Trump.

ABOUT THE AUTHOR

Donald J. Trump is the very definition of the American success story, continually setting the standards of excellence while expanding his interests in real estate, sports, and entertainment. He is the archetypal businessman—a deal-maker without peer.

Mr. Trump started his business career in an office he shared with his father in Sheepshead Bay, Brooklyn, New York. He worked with his father for five years, where they were busy making deals together. Mr. Trump has been quoted as saying, "My father was my mentor, and I learned a tremendous amount about every aspect of the construction industry from him." Likewise, Fred C. Trump often stated that "some of my best deals were made by my son, Donald . . . everything he touches seems to turn to gold." Mr. Trump then entered the very different world of Manhattan real estate.

In New York City and around the world, the Trump signature is synonymous with the most prestigious of addresses. Among them are the world-renowned Fifth Avenue skyscraper Trump Tower, and the luxury residential buildings Trump Parc, Trump Palace, Trump Plaza, 610 Park Avenue, the Trump World Tower (the tallest building on the East Side of Manhattan), and Trump

Park Avenue. Mr. Trump was also responsible for the designation and construction of the Jacob Javits Convention Center on land controlled by him, known as the West 34th Street Railroad Yards, and the total exterior restoration of the Grand Central Terminal as part of his conversion of the neighboring Commodore Hotel into the Grand Hyatt. The development is considered one of the most successful restorations in the city and earned Mr. Trump an award from Manhattan's Community Board Five for the "tasteful and creative recycling of a distinguished hotel." Over the years, Mr. Trump has owned and sold many great buildings in New York, including the Plaza Hotel (which he renovated and brought back to its original grandeur, as heralded by the *New York Times Magazine*), the Hotel St. Moritz (now called the Ritz-Carlton on Central Park South), and until 2002, the land under the Empire State Building (which allowed the land and lease to be merged together for the first time in more than 50 years). Additionally, the NikeTown store is owned by Mr. Trump, located on East 57th Street and adjacent to Tiffany's. In early 2008, Gucci opened their largest store in the world in Trump Tower.

In 1997, the Trump International Hotel & Tower opened its doors to the world. This 52-story mixed-use super-luxury hotel and residential building is located on the crossroads of Manhattan's West Side, on Central Park West at Columbus Circle. It was designed by the world-famous architect Philip Johnson and has achieved some of the highest sales prices and rentals in the United States. As one of only three hotels in the nation to have received a double *Forbes* Five-Star rating for both the hotel and its restaurant, Jean-Georges, it has also received the Five Star Diamond Award from the American Academy of Hospitality Sciences, and was voted the number one business hotel in New York City by *Travel + Leisure* magazine. *Condé Nast Traveler* magazine has named it the number one hotel in the US, and its innovative concept has been copied worldwide. It has won the *Forbes* Five-Star Hotel Award each year from 2009 to 2015 and ranked in the *Condé Nast Traveler* "Readers' Choice" awards every year since 2010. This year marks the eighteenth anniversary of this Trump Hotel Collection gem.

Mr. Trump was also the developer of the largest parcel of land in New York City, the former West Side Rail Yards, which is now Trump Place. On this 100-acre property, fronting along the Hudson River from 59th Street to 72nd Street, is the largest development ever approved by the New York City Planning Commission. There are a total of 16 buildings on the site, with Mr. Trump erecting the first nine buildings and the other portion of land being sold for a substantial amount. Mr. Trump also donated a 25-acre waterfront park on Trump Place and a 700-foot sculptured pier to the City of New York.

Other acquisitions in New York City include the Trump Building at 40 Wall Street, the landmark 1.3-million-square-foot, 72-story building located in Manhattan's Financial District, directly across from the New York Stock Exchange and the tallest building in downtown Manhattan after the new World Trade Center. This purchase, which occurred during the depths of the New York City real estate market, is said to be one of the best real estate deals made in the past 25 years and is considered to have one of the most beautiful "Tops" of any building in the country. In addition, Mr. Trump built 610 Park Avenue (at 64th Street), formerly known as the Mayfair Regent Hotel, which was very successfully converted into super-luxury condominium apartments achieving, at that time, the highest prices on Park Avenue. Further east, adjacent to the United Nations, sits the spectacular Trump World Tower, a 90-story luxury residential building and one of the tallest residential towers in the world. The Trump World Tower has received rave reviews from architecture critics, with Herbert Muschamp of the *New York Times* calling it "a handsome hunk of a glass tower." Likewise, Trump World Tower is considered one of the most successful condominium towers ever built in the United States.

In 2001, Mr. Trump announced plans for his first foray into Chicago, where he built the Trump International Hotel & Tower/Chicago. The 2.7-million-square-foot, 92-story mixed-use tower is located on the banks of the Chicago River, directly west of Michigan Avenue (the most prominent site in Chicago), and is one of the tallest residences in the world and the ninth-tallest building in the world. The architect is Skidmore, Owings & Merrill, Chicago, and the tower also includes four levels of retail shops. The hotel opened in January of 2008 to great acclaim, and in 2010 received *Travel + Leisure* magazine's award as the #1 Hotel in the US and Canada as well as their "World's Best Business Hotel" Award in 2014. *Condé Nast Traveler* has ranked the hotel in its "Readers' Choice Awards" every year since 2011. The hotel has earned Five-Star ratings for hotel and restaurant in the *Forbes* Travel Guide Awards in 2014 and 2015, and has been a AAA Five Diamond Hotel award winner since 2011.

In 2002, Mr. Trump purchased the fabled Delmonico Hotel, located at 59th Street and Park Avenue, and redeveloped it into a state-of-the-art luxury 35-story condominium named Trump Park Avenue. It was Mr. Trump's desire to make this one of the most luxurious buildings in New York City, which was achieved. Mr. Trump has been lauded by a multitude of publications for having retained the grandeur and charm of the building while incorporating 21st-century services and amenities. Mr. Trump is co-owner, with Vornado Realty Trust, of the iconic 555 California Street tower (the Bank of America Building) in San Francisco, one of the most important office buildings on the West Coast of the US, and the prized 1290 Avenue of the Americas building, one of New York's biggest buildings, with the largest office floor-plates in New York.

Mr. Trump's portfolio of holdings also includes Trump National Golf Club in Westchester, New York, a signature Fazio golf course and residential development, and a 250-acre estate known as the Mansion at Seven Springs, the former home of Katharine Graham (of *The Washington Post*), which will be developed into a world-class luxury housing development. Mr. Trump also purchased one of the largest parcels of land in California, which fronts on the Pacific Ocean. A Donald J. Trump championship golf course, called Trump National Golf Club/Los Angeles, has been built on this site, and it has been voted the number one golf course in California. Seventy-five luxury estates will follow. In addition, the Tom Fazio–designed Trump National Golf Club has been built in Lamington Farms in Bedminster, New Jersey, on the 525-acre Cowperthwaite Estate, considered to be the best in the state. An additional 18-hole course was opened recently. In November of 2008, Mr. Trump received approval to develop Trump International Golf Links Scotland, located in Aberdeen, Scotland, with more than three miles of spectacular ocean water-front (the North Sea). It opened on July 10 of 2012, and a second 18-hole course has been approved. In July 2013, *Golf Week* magazine named Trump International Golf Links Scotland "The Best Modern Day Golf Course in the World." In August of 2008, Mr. Trump purchased a golf course in Colts Neck, New Jersey, which is now Trump National Golf Club/Colts Neck, and in February of 2009 he bought an 800-acre parcel of land and club near Washington, DC, which fronts the Potomac River for three miles, to become Trump National Golf Club, Washington, DC. Two more golf courses were added to his portfolio in December of 2009, Trump National Golf Club—Philadelphia, and Trump National

Golf Club—Hudson Valley. In April of 2010, a new celebrity reality series, *Donald J. Trump's Fabulous World of Golf*, debuted on Golf Channel with great success.

In Palm Beach, Florida, Mr. Trump converted the famous and historic estate owned by Marjorie Merriweather Post and E. F. Hutton, Mar-a-Lago, into the private, ultra-luxury Mar-a-Lago Club. It received the award from the American Academy of Hospitality Sciences as the "Best Club Anywhere in the World." It was designated a National Historic Landmark in 1980, and Mar-a-Lago is often referred to as "The Jewel of Palm Beach." Also in Palm Beach and located seven minutes from Mar-a-Lago is the Trump International Golf Club. Designed by the famed golf course architect Jim Fazio, this $40 million golf course has magnificent tropical landscaping, water features, and streams and elevations of 100 feet (unprecedented in all of Florida). Opened in October 1999, this course has been acclaimed as one of the best in the United States. An additional nine-hole course was opened in 2006 to equal acclaim.

The Trump Hotel Collection was created to designate a new level of internationally important hotels, defined by elegance and attention to detail. One of the most elegant additions to the Las Vegas skyline is a super-luxury 60-story hotel condominium tower, the five-star Trump International Hotel Las Vegas. This hotel was named by *USA Today* as the "Best Bet in Vegas" in 2012 and was listed on *Travel + Leisure*'s list of "World's Best Business Hotel Awards" in 2011. Current and future developments in the Trump Hotel Collection include towers in SoHo/New York (which opened in spring of 2010 and made *Travel + Leisure* magazine's list of the best new hotels—the only one in New York to be included—as well as the AAA Five Diamond distinction in 2013 and 2014, and their "World's Best Business Hotel Awards: New York" in 2011), Chicago (opened 2008), Waikiki/Hawaii (opened November 2009 and received *Forbes* Travel Guide's Five-Star hotel rating in 2015), Panama (opened July 2011 and received the Luxury Travel Advisor's "Top 10 Luxury Hotel Openings" in 2011), Toronto (which received the *Forbes* Five-Star rating in 2014), Trump National Doral Miami (which completed its $250 million transformation in early 2015), and Trump International Golf Links & Hotel Ireland (a highly sought-after acquisition by the Trump Organization in 2014). International hotel developments as of 2015 include Baku, Azerbaijan (opened in June 2015); Vancouver, BC, and Rio de Janiero, both opening in 2016. Trump Towers, Istanbul, Şişli, combines two towers (one residential tower and one office tower), located in the vibrant Mecidiyeköy district.

In February of 2012, the Trump Organization was selected as the developer of the famous Old Post Office Building in Washington, DC. This building is considered a prized jewel, and competition for it was fierce. Plans include a 300-room super-luxury hotel, a museum gallery, and retaining the original exterior façade, doors, hallways, and other interior features. When completed, this hotel, which sits on Pennsylvania Avenue, will be one of the most luxurious in the world, and it is seen as a generational asset by the Trump family. Trump International Hotel Washington, DC, is slated to open in 2016.

In a departure from his real estate acquisitions, Mr. Trump and the NBC Television Network were partners in the ownership and broadcast rights for the three largest beauty competitions in the world: the Miss Universe, Miss USA, and Miss Teen USA pageants. Mr. Trump recently purchased the NBC portion and then sold the entire company to IMG. Trump Model Management, which was founded in 1999, has become one of the leading modeling agencies in New York City.

Mr. Trump rebuilt the Wollman Skating Rink in Central Park.

This project was particularly special to Mr. Trump. The city had been trying for seven years to rebuild and restore the rink, whereupon Mr. Trump interceded and restored the rink in four months at only $1.8 million of the city's $20 million cost. Similarly, he rebuilt Lasker Rink in Harlem, also located in Central Park, which has had great success as well. In addition, Mr. Trump is given credit for having made a major and very favorable impact on the economy of the city by creating the condominium boom, versus the co-ops that were more prevalent in the past.

An accomplished author, Mr. Trump's 1987 autobiography, *The Art of the Deal*, became one of the most successful business bestsellers of all time, having sold in excess of four million copies, and being a *New York Times* number one bestseller for many weeks. The sequel, *Surviving at the Top*, was on the *New York Times* bestseller list and was also a number one bestseller, as was his third book, *The Art of the Comeback*. Mr. Trump's fourth book, *The America We Deserve*, was a departure from his past literary efforts. This book deals with issues most important to the American people today and focuses on his views regarding American political, economic, and social problems. His fifth book, *How to Get Rich: Big Deals from the Star of* The Apprentice, became an immediate bestseller on all lists, as did *Trump: The Way to the Top* and *Trump: Think Like a Billionaire,* which was released in October 2004. *Trump: The Best Golf Advice I Ever Received* was published in April 2005, followed by *Trump: The Best Real Estate Advice I Ever Received* in 2006. He has also teamed up with Robert Kiyosaki to make publishing history with their book *Why We Want You to Be Rich: Two Men, One Message,* which in October of 2006 made the #1 spot on the *New York Times,* the *Wall Street Journal*, and Amazon bestseller lists. *Trump 101: The Way to Success* debuted in late 2006. In October of 2007 Mr. Trump's book with Bill Zanker, *Think Big,* was launched. In early 2008, Mr.

Trump's *Never Give Up* was released, followed by *Think Like a Champion* in April of 2009. *Midas Touch,* another collaboration with Robert Kiyosaki, was released in October of 2011. *Time to Get Tough: Making America #1 Again* was released in early December of 2011, becoming a bestseller.

A native of New York City, Mr. Trump is a graduate of the Wharton School of Finance, and in 1984, he won the Entrepreneur of the Year award from the Wharton School. Involved in numerous civic and charitable organizations, he is a member of the Board of Directors for the Police Athletic League. Mr. Trump also serves as Chairman of the Donald J. Trump Foundation as well as Co-Chairman of the New York Vietnam Veteran's Memorial Fund. In 1995, he served as the Grand Marshal of the largest parade ever held in New York, the Nation's Parade, which celebrated the 50th anniversary of the end of World War II. In 2002, Mr. Trump received an honor from the USO for his efforts on behalf of the US Armed Forces. He also hosts the annual Red Cross Ball at his Mar-a-Lago Club in Palm Beach. In January of 2012, he received the American Cancer Society Lifetime Achievement Award. In April of 2015, Mr. Trump received the Commandant's Leadership Award from the Marine Corps–Law Enforcement Foundation, given to him by General Joseph F. Dunford, Jr., the Chairman of the Joint Chiefs of Staff.

Mr. Trump is a founding member of both the Committee to Complete Construction of the Cathedral of St. John the Divine and The Wharton School Real Estate Center. Mr. Trump was also a committee member of the Celebration of Nations commemorating the 50th anniversary of the United Nations and UNICEF. He was also designated "The Developer of the Year" by the Construction Management Association of America and Master Builder by the New York State Office of Parks, Recreational & Historic Preservation. In June 2000, Mr. Trump received his greatest honor of all, the Hotel and Real Estate Visionary of the Century, given by the UJA Federation, and in 2003 was named to the Benefactors Board of Directors by the Historical Society of Palm Beach County. In 2007, he was awarded the "Green Space" Award by the friends of Westchester County Parks, as he donated 436 acres of land in Westchester, New York, to create the Donald J. Trump State Park.

By January of 2004, Mr. Trump had joined forces with Mark Burnett Productions and NBC to produce and star in the television reality show *The Apprentice*. This quickly became the number one show on television, making ratings history and receiving rave reviews. The first season finale had the highest ratings on television that year after the Superbowl, with 28 million people watching. Few shows have garnered the worldwide attention that *The Apprentice* has achieved, including three Emmy nominations. In 2007, a *New York Times* article quoted NBC's president, Ben Silverman, as saying *The Apprentice* "has been the most successful reality series ever on NBC." *The Celebrity Apprentice* has met with great success as well, being one of the highest-rated shows on television. The *Apprentice* series ran for a landmark 14 seasons. In 2005, Mr. Trump hosted *Saturday Night Live,* which resulted in one of their highest ratings of the year. Moreover, he is producing additional network and cable television programming via his Los Angeles–based production company, Trump Productions LLC. His radio program with Clear Channel Radio, parent company of Premiere Radio Networks, beginning in the summer of 2004, was a wonderful success.

In the August 21–28, 2006, issue of *BusinessWeek* magazine, Mr. Trump was voted, by its readers, as "the world's most competitive businessperson" and voted by the staff and writers of *BusinessWeek* as one of the Top 10 most competitive businesspeople in the world. The ongoing business success of the Trump

Organization was recognized by the *Crain's New York Business List 2012*, with a ranking of Number 1 for the largest privately held company in New York. Also renowned for his celebrity status, *Forbes* ranked Mr. Trump as one of the top celebrities in the world. Mr. Trump is one of only two people (the other being Hillary Clinton) named to ABC's Barbara Walters special *The Most Fascinating People* two times, most recently on her 2011 show.

Mr. Trump is one of the highest-paid speakers in the world, often drawing tens of thousands of people. In September of 2011, Mr. Trump gave a two-city speech in Australia, for more than $5 million and has been paid tens of millions of dollars for speeches made over his career. In October of 2012, Mr. Trump spoke in London at the National Achievers Congress. In January of 2007, Mr. Trump received a star on the Hollywood Walk of Fame, and in 2008, "You're fired!" was listed as the #3 greatest TV catchphrase of all time, led only by "Here's Johnnny" and "One small step for man . . ." In March of 2013, Mr. Trump was inducted into the WWE Hall of Fame in front of 25,000 fans at Madison Square Garden. The reasons for this great honor were that he held two of the most successful WrestleMania events ever—but of even greater importance, he and Vince McMahon were involved in the WrestleMania 23 "Battle of the Billionaires" in 2007 in Detroit Stadium, which to this day is the highest-rated show and the highest dollar amount on pay-per-view in the history of wrestling. In April of 2013, the *New York Observer* named Mr. Trump as #1 in its Power 100 Readers Poll. Also in April of 2013, Mr. Trump spoke at the annual Lincoln dinner in Michigan, which was the largest Lincoln dinner in their 124-year history and the largest Lincoln event in our country's history where a US president was not the speaker. In 2013, Mr. Trump received the T. Boone Pickens Award from *The American Spectator* at the Robert L. Bartley Gala. The highly respected writer Joe Queenan, after hearing Mr. Trump speak at a Learning Annex event in 2006, wrote that the $30 million he was paid for his appearances may have been an underpayment.

On the *Larry King Show* in June 2008, Barbara Corcoran, a well-respected real estate expert, said, "How can I possibly compete with Donald Trump? Thanks to him I sold more property in Manhattan. He single-handedly turned the whole image of Manhattan around in the 1980s, when nobody wanted to live in New York." Robert Kiyosaki, author of *Rich Dad, Poor Dad*, added, "Donald is the smartest man in real estate—no one else even comes close." In an article in the *New York Times* in November of 2013, Arthur Zeckendorf, a New York City developer of ultra-luxury condominiums, was asked who most influenced him in the industry: "I think Donald Trump. He basically started the high-end condo business. I certainly followed him, admired him." When asked specifically what he learned: "That building great condos is an art, and you really have to make the product the best out there."

In July of 2008, Mr. Trump sold an estate that he purchased (a short time earlier) for $40 million at 515 South Ocean Boulevard in Palm Beach for a record-setting price of $100 million, and in March of 2010, the penthouse apartment at Trump International Hotel & Tower in New York City sold for $33 million. In May of 2011, Mr. Trump purchased the Kluge Estate and Vineyard in Charlottesville, Virginia, now the Trump Vineyard Estates. It is the largest vineyard on the East Coast.

In February of 2012, Mr. Trump purchased the iconic 800-acre Doral Hotel & Country Club in Miami, which includes five championship golf courses, the world-renowned Blue Monster championship golf course, a 50,000-square-foot spa, and a 700-room hotel. It is home to the Cadillac World Championship of Golf. In April 2012, Mr. Trump purchased the Point Lake & Golf Club in North Carolina, which has become Trump National

Golf Club, Charlotte, and in December 2012 he purchased the Ritz Carlton Golf Club in Jupiter, Florida, which is now Trump National Golf Club, Jupiter. In April 2013, Trump International Golf Club, Dubai, was announced, and the Trump Estates, which includes more than 100 luxury villas overlooking the golf course, were released for sale in March of 2014. Trump Golf Links at Ferry Point, Bronx, New York City, opened in May of 2015. As Jack Nicklaus said, "Trump has been very, very good with getting things done with the city. I think he pushed it over the edge. He did a really good job of getting it to the finish line." The club was under construction for several decades, with more than $200 million in taxpayer money being wasted. When Mr. Trump got involved, it was completed in one year and designed by Jack Nicklaus. All are destined to become great additions to a burgeoning golf course and club portfolio.

In February of 2014, Mr. Trump announced that he had purchased the Doonbeg Golf Resort in Ireland, which will become Trump International Golf Links and Hotel, Ireland. This 450-acre property fronts on the Atlantic Ocean in County Clare. It is now being totally redeveloped by Mr. Trump. In April 2014, Mr. Trump purchased the famed Turnberry Resort in Scotland, home of the Open Championship. Located on more than 1,000 acres, and on the Irish Sea and Isle of Arran, many consider the Championship Course to be #1 in the world. In addition, in April of 2014, the PGA of America announced that the 2022 PGA Championship would be hosted by Trump National Golf Club, Bedminster, and that the 2017 Senior PGA Championship would be held at Trump National Golf Club, Washington, DC. It was announced in October of 2014 that the Trump World Golf Club Dubai, an 18-hole championship course, will be designed by Tiger Woods. The Women's British Open 2015 was held at Trump Turnberry in July of 2015.

Mr. Trump has recently been recognized by *Golf Digest* magazine as "Golf's Greatest Builder Today" and by *Sports Illustrated* as "The Most Important Figure in the World of Golf." Brian Morgan, the world's leading golf photographer, has stated, "Donald Trump has the greatest collection of golf courses and clubs ever built or assembled by one man."

On June 16, 2015, Mr. Trump officially announced his candidacy for the presidency of the United States.

**Some of the properties owned and/or developed and managed
or licensed by Donald J. Trump and The Trump Organization**

- Trump Tower
- Trump World Tower
- Trump Parc
- Trump Parc East
- Trump Park Avenue
- Trump Palace
- Trump Place
- 610 Park Avenue
- Trump Plaza
- Trump International Hotel &
  Tower New York
- Trump International Hotel &
  Tower Chicago
- Trump International Hotel
  Las Vegas
- Trump International Golf
  Links, Aberdeen (Hotel +
  Golf)
- Trump International Golf
  Links & Hotel, Doonbeg,
  Ireland (Hotel + Golf)
- Trump Turnberry, Scotland
  (Hotel + Golf)
- Trump International Hotel,
  Washington DC (*Trump was
  awarded the contract through
  the GSA as the preferred
  developer of the iconic
  Old Post Office. This was
  considered one of the most*

*highly sought-after projects in
GSA history.*)

- Trump International Golf
  Club, Palm Beach
- Trump National Golf Club,
  Jupiter
- Trump National Golf Club,
  Washington, DC
- Trump National Doral,
  Miami (Hotel + Golf)
- Trump National Golf Club,
  Colts Neck
- Trump National Golf Club,
  Westchester
- Trump National Golf Club,
  Hudson Valley
- Trump National Golf Club,
  Bedminster
- Trump National Golf Club,
  Philadelphia
- Trump National Golf Club,
  Los Angeles
- Trump National Golf Club,
  Charlotte
- Trump Golf Links at
  Ferry Point (developer and
  operator)
- The Albemarle Estate at
  Trump Winery
- Trump Vineyard Estates

- The Mar-a-Lago Club
- The Estates at Trump National, LA
- Le Chateau Des Palmiers, St. Martin
- Trump Seven Springs, Bedford, NY
- Townhouses adjacent to Trump Plaza New York City
- Two private homes in Palm Beach adjacent to The Mar-a-Lago Club
- Private home in Beverly Hills
- 40 Wall Street
- Trump Tower
- NikeTown
- 1290 Avenue of the Americas in partnership with Vornado
- 555 California Street in partnership with Vornado
- Two shopping centers in New York City
- Trump Tower Mumbai, India
- Trump Towers Pune, India
- Trump Towers Istanbul
- Trump Tower Punta del Este
- Trump Tower at Century City, Philippines
- Trump Hollywood
- Trump International Beach Resort, Miami
- Trump Towers Sunny Isles
- The Estates at Trump International Golf Club, Dubai
- Trump Hotel Rio de Janiero
- Trump International Hotel & Tower Waikiki
- Trump Ocean Club, Panama
- Trump International Hotel & Tower Vancouver
- Trump International Hotel & Tower Toronto
- Trump SoHo New York
- Trump Tower at City Center
- Trump Plaza New Rochelle
- Trump Parc Stamford
- Trump Park Residences Yorktown
- Trump Plaza Residences Jersey City
- Recently announced hotel developments in Lido & Bali
- Trump World Golf Club, Dubai

- Trump International Golf Club, Dubai

- Mr. Trump also operates the iconic Wollman Rink, the Lasker Rink, and the landmark Carousel, all located in Central Park.

Corporate Aircrafts owned by Donald J. Trump

- Boeing 757
- Cessna Citation X
- 3 Sikorsky 76 Helicopters